Helga & Paul Smith
Bernhard Förth

On The Backside, Please!

Wenn Übersetzungen nach hinten losgehen!

Arcos Verlag

A One-Word-A-Day Product©
www.owad.de

Bibliografische Information der Deutschen Bibliothek
Die Deutsche Bibliothek verzeichnet diese Publikation in der Deutschen Nationalbibliografie; detaillierte bibliografische Daten sind im Internet über http://dnb.dbb.de abrufbar

Satz und Herstellung: Dominik Angerbauer, Sebastian Jopen; Bosch-Druck
Umschlaggestaltung: Bernhard Förth
Druck und Bindung: Bosch-Druck, Landshut

ISBN: 3-935339-15-1

1. Auflage 2004

www.arcos-verlag.de

to

Dr. Harald Oster

"Let us once!"

Dieses Buch enthält:

Die englische Übersetzung “If you have nothing on, …” (Wenn Sie nichts vor haben, …) klingt sehr interessant auf deutsch!

Wenn Sie nichts anhaben, lesen Sie ruhig weiter ...

Eine amerikanische Diplomatengattin, die einige Jahre ihres Lebens dem Studium der deutschen Sprache gewidmet hatte, lud deutsche Gäste zum Cocktail ein. Einer der angesehenen Gäste bedankte sich beim Abschied für den gelungenen Abend und schloss mit den Worten:

„Ich hoffe, dass wir uns bald wiedersehen". „Gerne", antwortete die charmante Gastgeberin und fügte in (fast) perfektem Deutsch hinzu:
„Kommen Sie doch mal vorbei, wenn Sie nichts anhaben."

Diese im Englischen völlig unverfängliche Einladung –
"If you have nothing on" – *(Wenn Sie nichts anderes vorhaben ...)* klingt in der wörtlichen Übersetzung jedoch etwas irreführend.

So sind viele dieser Übersetzungsfehler amüsant, ohne dass sich gravierende Missverständnisse daraus ergeben können, wie auch der „Faux Pas" des deutschsprachigen Geschäftsmannes, der nach erfolgreichem Vertragsabschluss seinen Partner auffordert:
"Please sign on the backside"
*(Bitte unterschreiben Sie auf dem Hintern)**

Trotzdem können wir in diesem Fall nur hoffen, dass dieser Englisch sprechende Gesprächspartner auch den viel gepriesenen englischen Humor besitzt und die Aufforderung nicht allzu wörtlich nimmt.

Das **eigentliche Handicap** bei den o.g. amüsanten Missverständnissen ist aber, dass die meisten „Native Speaker" aus Gründen der Höflichkeit davon Abstand nehmen, die Übersetzungsfehler ihres Gegenübers zu korrigieren.

* Korrekt wäre = "Please sign on the other side" or "Please sign on the reverse"

Zuerst die „Good News"

Für Deutschsprachige sind die GOOD NEWS, dass viele englische Worte den deutschen ähnlich oder sogar gleichbedeutend sind: Hand, Finger, Arm, ... Kinn, Nase, Lippen, ... usw. Der geniale Trick, deutsche Worte mit einem englischen Akzent auszusprechen, wird Ihnen da des Öfteren gute Dienste leisten - besonders bei Begriffen oder Fachausdrücken, die vom Lateinischen abgeleitet werden:

Abakus = abacus
Abstinenz = abstinence
Adamsapfel = Adam's apple
Amortisation = amortisation
Amnestie = amnesty
Anekdote = anecdote
arrogant = arrogant
ästhetisch = aesthetic
...

Ihr Englisch ist besser als Sie denken. Weil Sie deutsch sprechen, haben Sie automatisch Zugriff auf Tausende wertvoller Worte. Sammeln Sie diese Worte, lernen Sie ihre Aussprache und benutzen Sie sie.

Eine Liste dieser „Instant words" dieses Buches können Sie ebenfalls als kostenfreies Hörbeispiel herunterladen von unserer One-Word-A-Day website at: www.owad.de

„Instant English" Wörter sind einfach zu lernen, einfach zu benutzen, so lange Sie die folgenden „Bad News" berücksichtigen.

... die „Bad News" über Englisch

Leider haben nicht alle Wörter, die ähnlich oder gleich klingen, im englischen die bedeutung, auf die man im Deutschen schließen würde. Es gibt ungefähr 100 häufig benutzte Wörter, die nicht so einfach zu übersetzen sind:

Gesicht ist nicht „sight" sondern „face"; Bein ist nicht „bone" sondern „leg", und Körper ist nicht „corpse" sondern „body". Können Sie sich vorstellen, was es für eine Wirkung hätte, Ihrem Partner/Ihrer Partnerin in einem romantischen Moment zuzuflüstern, er/sie habe „a lovely corpse!" (corpse = Leiche)?

Aber genau hierbei ergibt sich auch die beste Gelegenheit diese Sprachfallen ausfindig zu machen. Stellen Sie sich einfach ein amüsantes, einprägsames Bild des möglichen Missverständnisses vor, und Sie werden es nie mehr vergessen! Die Illustrationen von Bernhard Förth, die wir in diesem Buch verteilt haben, zeigen, wie leicht solche Visualisierungen aussehen könnten.

Zwei Tipps zur schnellen Erweiterung Ihres Englischvokabulars:

1. Identifizieren und visualisieren Sie die 100 häufigsten Übersetzungsfehler und prägen Sie sich gleichzeitig die korrekte Version ein.

2. Sammeln Sie systematisch „Instant"-Wörter beim Lesen oder Zuhören und benutzen Sie diese aktiv (beim Sprechen und Schreiben).

Quiz

1. At the Fitness Center

1. I have a **provisional** appointment with my instructor. But I can't confirm until I'm sure that I've found exactly the right outfit.

2. Someone should take all the heat that we **generate** on the running machines and sell it to an electricity company. Then our membership charges wouldn't have to be so high.

3. Not everyone agrees with me, but I think Herman doing handstands in the sauna is a **flagrant** abuse of the club rules.

4. Marcello has a very **paradoxical** attitude about his health. Yesterday, I saw him weightlifting with a cigarette in his mouth.

5. I'm so excited! Ronaldo visited my fitness center yesterday and gave me a signed photo of himself. When looked at it later, I saw I'd also got three kisses from him on the **backside**.

Lösung

	ENGLISCH		DEUTSCH
1	provisional	=	provisorisch
2	generate	=	generieren
3	flagrant	=	flagrant
4	paradoxical	=	paradox
5	backside	≠	die Rückseite
	backside	=	das Hinterteil
	the reverse (side) **the other side, the back**	=	**die Rückseite**

Richtig wäre:

I'm so excited! Ronaldo visited my fitness center yesterday and gave me a signed photo of himself. When I looked at it later, I saw I'd also got three kisses from him on the **reverse**.

2. Ouch, that hurt!

1. "There needs to be a better **demarcation** of our roles. Why don't I concentrate on winning the big deals, while you spend time looking for another job?"

2. "Do you think this dress would be suitable for the gala dinner? Tell me the truth." "Well, to be brutally honest, it makes you look a bit **thick**."

3. "The standard of **debate** at this conference could not have been higher - unless some interesting and intelligent people had attended."

4. "It's really hard to dislike the leader of the national **coalition**, but it is well worth making the effort."

5. "I think we can all agree that we've heard some excellent **arguments** for increasing military expenditure, but sadly the ones we heard today were not among them."

Lösung

	ENGLISCH		DEUTSCH
1	demarcation	=	die Demarkation (Abgrenzung, Grenzziehung)
2	thick	≠	dick
3	debate	=	die Debatte
4	coalition	=	die Koalition
5	arguments	=	die Argumente
	thick	=	dumm
	fat, overweight	=	**dick**

Richtig wäre:

"Do you think this dress would be suitable for the gala dinner? Tell me the truth."

"Well, to be brutally honest, it makes you look a bit **fat**."

3. Reputation management

1. I just lost my job at Happy Travel Adventures. The boss said I was too **pessimistic**. I always knew that was going to happen.

2. People say that my colourful English comes across as **ordinary**.

3. Some people say that I'm too **phlegmatic**. But it doesn't bother me.

4. "I am very **direct**" she said bluntly, proving her point.

5. It's absolutely ridiculous for anyone to suggest that I'm **dogmatic**. I'm a great team player, and my opinion on this, as with everything else, will not be changed.

Lösung

	ENGLISCH		DEUTSCH
1	pessimistic	=	pessimistisch
2	ordinary	≠	ordinär
3	phlegmatic	=	phlegmatisch, stoisch
4	direct	=	direkt
5	dogmatic	=	dogmatisch, rechthaberisch
	ordinary	=	gewöhnlich, üblich, normal
	vulgar, common, uncouth	=	**ordinär**

Richtig wäre:

People say that my colourful English comes across as **vulgar**.

4. Political confusion

1. I asked my professor why there was so much political **apathy** in democratic countries. She said it was because the majority of people thought their vote didn't make a difference.

2. "I think **anarchy** would be so cool," said Clare. "I'd vote for any government who supported that system."

3. Shortly after starting university, Craig told me he believed in Marxist **ideology**. By Christmas he was a Social Democrat and now he says he's a Conservative.

4. Our president says she is trying to **balance** the country's finances. I think this means that every time her government spends a dollar, it must also borrow a dollar!

5. The Greek Ambassador wished he hadn't worn **a smoking** to the summer garden party when the other guests started asking him to re-fill their wine glasses.

Lösung

	ENGLISCH		DEUTSCH
1	apathy	=	die Apathie
2	anarchy	=	die Anarchie
3	ideology	=	die Ideologie
4	balance	=	balancieren bei Finanzen: ausgleichen
5	a smoking	≠	der Smoking
	a smoking	=	!?! (wird nicht verstanden)
	dinner jacket (UK), tuxedo (USA)	=	**der Smoking**

Richtig wäre:

The Greek Ambassador wished he hadn't worn **a dinner jacket** to the summer garden party when the other guests started asking him to re-fill their wine glasses.

5. Better luck next time

1. People told me that I had written the **ultimate** book on self-publishing. The sales figures told a different story.

2. I'm frightened of water, so I asked the boat captain if there was another way to reach the island. "Yes," he said. "Just wait until it's your turn for **reincarnation** and ask to come back as something with wings."

3. Our team manager, Ms Baker, promised to reward me if I performed well at work this year. I couldn't believe it when she called Gordon into her office and gave him the **gratification** that should have been mine.

4. It was a beautiful evening of moonlight and romance. If he only hadn't told me that **anecdote** about the kangaroo and the Governor of Wumbarama City, I think we might still be together today.

5. The pop singer's first song made him an overnight **sensation**. Unfortunately, he was forgotten by the next evening.

Lösung

	ENGLISCH		DEUTSCH
1	ultimate	=	ultimativ
2	reincarnation	=	die Reinkarnation
3	gratification	≠	die Gratifikation
4	anecdote	=	die Anekdote
5	sensation	=	die Sensation
	gratification	=	die Befriedigung, die Erfüllung,die Freude
	bonus	=	**die Gratifikation**

Richtig wäre:

Our team manager, Ms Baker, promised to reward me if I performed well at work this year. I couldn't believe it when she called Gordon into her office and gave him the **bonus** that should have been mine.

The word "backside" reminds English speakers of "das Hinterteil" – they'll smile politely but seldom correct you. It's safer to sign on the "reverse" or on the "back".

"Undertaker" is very serious profession (Leichenbestatter). Sometimes French is the language of choice in the US & UK – translate "Unternehmer" as "entrepreneur".

6. Affairs of state

1. "I would not be standing here today, without the love and support of **my woman**," said the new president. And he should have added that having a multi-millionaire father was quite useful too.

2. The foreign ambassador was famous for being **eloquent**. Unfortunately, the translator lost his voice and we weren't able to appreciate it.

3. "I believe in **pluralism**," said the president. "This means I make the decisions, and you play your part by agreeing with them."

4. The problem with our **immigration** policy is not that it lets too many people in, but that it doesn't encourage certain people to leave.

5. "We find it strange," said the defence minister, "that the most violent opposition to our plan for military action has come from the **pacifists**."

Lösung

	ENGLISCH		DEUTSCH
1	my woman	≠	meine Frau
2	eloquent	=	eloquent
3	pluralism	=	der Pluralismus
4	immigration	=	die Immigration
5	pacifists	=	die Pazifisten
	my woman*	=	Sklavin
	my wife	=	**meine Frau**

* (rather disrespectful – and would certainly not be "politically correct")

Richtig wäre:

"I would not be standing here today, without the love and support of **my wife**," said the new president. And he should have added that having a multi-millionaire father was quite useful, too.

7. Good answers

1. My careers teacher said she thought I was too **subjective** in my arguments to become a lawyer. "Is that a fact?" I said.

2. I asked my professor if a system of extreme **capitalism** could ever be a success. He replied: "Tell me how much my answer is worth to you, and I'll tell you if I'm willing to sell it to you at that price."

3. I liked Gandhi's **comment**, when asked what he thought of Western civilization. He said: "I think it would be a good idea."

4. When someone warns me that this thing or that thing *can* be **fatal**, I always say: "Well, living is *definitely* fatal but that has never stopped anyone doing it."

5. A female politician once said to Winston Churchill: "If you were my husband, I'd put **gift** in your tea." To which he replied: "If you were my wife, I'd drink it.

Lösung

	ENGLISCH		DEUTSCH
1	subjective	=	subjektiv
2	capitalism	=	der Kapitalismus
3	comment	=	der Kommentar
4	fatal	=	fatal
5	gift	≠	das Gift
	gift	=	das Geschenk
	poison	=	**das Gift**

Richtig wäre:

A female politician once said to Winston Churchill: "If you were my husband, I'd put **poison** in your tea." To which he replied: "If you were my wife, I'd drink it."

8. More good answers

1. "This is going to sound like a terrible **cliché**, but how does it feel to be the most attractive person in the room."
   "You'll never know."

2. "I've got two tickets for an **exclusive** party in Hollywood. Would you like to go?"
   "Only if I can have both tickets."

3. "That **arrogant**-looking guy at the bar said he'd like to join us. What should I say?"
   "Tell him to go back to his planet because ours is full."

4. "What would you say if I said I wanted more than a **platonic** friendship with you?"
   "Nothing. I can't talk and laugh at the same time."

5. "My doctor had to give me a **recipe** to stop me dreaming about you every night."
   "Really? Too bad you didn't take an overdose."

Lösung

	ENGLISCH		DEUTSCH
1	cliché	=	das Klischee
2	exclusive	=	exklusiv
3	arrogant	=	arrogant
4	platonic	=	platonisch
5	recipe	≠	das Rezept (med.)
	recipe	=	das Kochrezept
	prescription	=	**das Rezept (med.)**

Richtig wäre:

"My doctor had to give me a **prescription** to stop me dreaming about you every night."
"Really? Too bad you didn't take an overdose."

9. News headlines

1. DISNEYLAND DESERVES **AUTONOMOUS** GOVERNMENT, SAYS MICKEY MOUSE
   Pluto claims real world "**indifferent** to our needs"

2. BEES TO **LOBBY** FOR SHORTER WORKING WEEK
   Queen says action is **heresy**

3. ELEPHANTS TELL FASHION DESIGNERS: "DON'T **IGNORE** LARGER SIZES"
   Cows add their voices in **solidarity**

4. CHAMELEON BECOMES ANIMAL WORLD'S FIRST **DRESSMAN**
   My natural ability to look good in different outfits could be **rentable**, he tells interviewer.

5. CATS **MOBILISE** TO START OWN CREAM FACTORY
   Fat-free milk served by humans is "a **travesty**"

Lösung

	ENGLISCH		DEUTSCH
1	autonomous indifferent	= =	autonom indifferent (Gleichgültig)
2	lobby heresy	= =	die Lobby die Häresie (Irrlehre)
3	ignore solidarity	= =	ignorieren die Solidarität
4	dressman rentable	≠ ≠	Dressman rentabel
5	mobilise travesty	= =	mobilisieren die Travestie (Zerrbild)
	dressman	=	? – Könnte als Transvestit interpretiert werden
	rentable	=	zu vermieten
	male model	=	**Dressman**
	profitable, cost-effective	=	**rentabel**

Richtig wäre:

CHAMELEON BECOMES ANIMAL WORLD'S FIRST **MALE MODEL**
My natural ability to look good in different outfits could be **profitable**, he tells interviewer.

10. On Main Street

1. This city has a real **transient** population. The Greek cafe on Fourth and Main was bought by an Italian family in February but when I stopped by for a cappuccino the other day, the Turk behind the counter said Senor Fabrizzi had moved to Las Vegas. I got a Turkish coffee instead.

2. A **discrepancy** on the bill meant I got a Versace suit for $100. So I spent the saving on a pair of Manolo Blahnik shoes.

3. They chose that **menu** at Brasserie Joe because it looked like good value. But it tasted like paper and I had to spend the money I saved on tablets to settle my stomach.

4. Our local grocery store announced an **embargo** on Slovakian tuna fish and Icelandic mango fruits ... on April 1.

5. The new bookstore next to the market has every **genre** of book imaginable - and some that I could never have imagined, such as Animal Autobiography and Feminist Archaeological Romance.

Lösung

	ENGLISCH		DEUTSCH
1	transient	=	transient, vergänglich
2	discrepancy	=	die Diskrepanz (Nichtübereinstimmung)
3	menu	≠	das Menü
4	embargo	=	das Embargo
5	genre	=	das Genre
	menu	=	die Speisekarte
	main meal, meal of the day, a list of dishes comprising a meal	=	**das Menü**

Richtig wäre:

They chose that **meal** at Brasserie Joe because it looked like good value. But it tasted like paper and I had to spend the money I saved on tablets to settle my stomach.

Be careful with "aufstehen". In the context of beds and early morning rising this mistake could easily raise a few eyebrows! "Er steht früh auf" = "He gets up early".

In Britain, a "bureau" is still an elegant piece of furniture - difficult to fit a businessman into it, but not impossible. Most people prefer to work in "offices".

11. Holiday hell

1. My return ticket was **guilty** for two months but I went home after just one week. Why didn't anyone tell me that a holiday in Venice is not suitable for someone who doesn't like water?

2. The trip was a **fiasco** from start to finish. The airline lost our luggage, the taxi took us to the wrong town, and when we finally got to the hotel, I discovered my ex-husband was staying in the next room.

3. We chose the villa because the travel agency said there was a fantastic **panorama** from the terrace. I'm sure the green fields and hills looked great – but they have been covered since 1998 in Europe's largest industrial park.

4. They described our holiday villa as **rustic**. The cold shower and hard beds were bad enough but finding three hungry sheep at the breakfast table was really too much.

5. I know there's a **risk** in doing winter sports. But how I could break both my legs and my nose I'll never know – especially as I was in the restaurant at the time.

Lösung

	ENGLISCH		DEUTSCH
1	guilty	≠	gültig
2	fiasco	=	das Fiasko
3	panorama	=	das Panorama
4	rustic	=	rustikal
5	risk	=	das Risiko
	guilty	=	schuldig
	valid, in effect, in force	=	**gültig**

Richtig wäre:

My return ticket was **valid** for two months but I went home after just one week. Why didn't anyone tell me that a holiday in Venice is not suitable for someone who doesn't like water?

12. When I was young, I thought like a child: now I'm old, I still do

1. I listen to the radio at 7am every morning to get the **actual** financial news. If my stocks have lost value, I ask Mommy for a bag of gummy bears to make me feel happy again.

2. There is not a **fragment** of truth in what he says. Father Christmas *is* real. How do I know? Because the Easter rabbit told me.

3. This is my business **maxim**: get to work early, have three great ideas before lunch, and eat chocolate cake for tea.

4. I try to travel by train whenever possible. It's not for **ecological** reasons, it's because sometimes I get to sit next to the driver.

5. Of course **philanthropy** is important in this company. Every year, we give 1 percent of our profits to a fund for poor families and 2 percent the Teddy Bear hospital.

Lösung

	ENGLISCH		DEUTSCH
1	actual	≠	aktuell
2	fragment	=	das Fragment (Bruchteil)
3	maxim	=	die Maxime
4	ecological	=	ökologisch
5	philanthropy	=	die Philanthropie (Menschenliebe)
	actual	=	eigentlich, tatsächlich, wirklich
	current, topical, up-to-date	=	**aktuell**

Richtig wäre:

I listen to the radio at 7am every morning to get the **current** financial news. If my stocks have lost value, I ask Mommy for a bag of gummy bears to make me feel happy again.

13. New kid on the block

1. Mr Miller has made me his **protégé**; he says I must listen, watch and learn everything I can from him. I think the most difficult thing will be learning to get food on my tie at every meal.

2. I didn't want to **blame** myself on my first day at college, so I said as little as possible. Unfortunately, the two things I did say were both wrong.

3. It's not easy to **adapt** to working life after being a student. Getting up at 7am makes me feel like I've moved to a different time zone from my friends. I think I've still got jet-lag!

4. His first week at Jones & Co has been a great success. He's been polite, friendly and has asked some very intelligent questions. But he is my son, so perhaps I'm not being completely **objective** here.

5. We have to sing the company song every morning, eat together every lunchtime, and do aerobics for 10 minutes before we go home. It feels like I've joined a **sect** not an advertising agency.

Lösung

	ENGLISCH		DEUTSCH
1	protégé	=	der Protegé (Schützling)
2	blame	≠	blamieren
3	adapt	=	adaptieren
4	objective	=	objektiv
5	sect	=	die Sekte
	blame	=	beschuldigen, tadeln, vorwerfen
	embarrass, disgrace oneself	=	**blamieren**

Richtig wäre:

I didn't want to **embarrass** myself on my first day at college, so I said as little as possible.
Unfortunately, the two things I did say were both wrong.

14. Bad answers

1. Derek asked me to provide him with an **alibi** for Saturday night, but I had to tell him that unfortunately I'd already promised to do the same thing for his wife.

2. "Can you confirm that your company is free from **nepotism**."
"I'm not sure, I'll have to ask my Dad. He's the boss."

3. What's wrong with my husband? When I suggested that a **preservative** might make sex last a little longer, he said:
"Yes, that's another reason I don't want to use one."

4. The debating society asked me to leave because they said it was obvious I didn't enjoy **conflict**. I had to agree with them.

5. I've no idea why my wife is so upset today. She simply asked if I'd heard of the **emancipation** of women, and I said "no", but that she could tell me all about it when she'd finished making supper.

Lösung

	ENGLISCH		DEUTSCH
1	alibi	=	das Alibi
2	nepotism	=	der Nepotismus (Vetternwirtschaft)
3	preservative	≠	das Präservativ
4	conflict	=	der Konflikt
5	emancipation	=	die Emanzipation
	preservative	=	das Konservierungsmittel
	condom, contraceptive	=	**das Präservativ, Kondom**

Richtig wäre:

What's wrong with my husband? When I suggested that a **condom** might make sex last a little longer, he said:
"Yes, that's another reason I don't want to use one."

15. Class action

1. Our school is having its annual **inspection** next week. I told all the teachers that they must be here – but after seeing Mr Hunt's last geography lesson I think it would be better if some of them stayed at home!

2. Most of the children are very **brave** when eating their school dinners. But when the cook tried to serve them raw green tomatoes they threw them around the room.

3. I asked my class to list their "10 Favourite Britons" in **chronological** order. I was so happy when I found that little Emma Jones had put me on her list, then I saw she'd put me *before* Queen Victoria.

4. The headmaster informed the newspaper that he didn't **accept** violence in his school … he was just powerless to stop it.

5. I told Maria that the **caricature** she had drawn of Claudia Schiffer for her art exam was really excellent, especially the way she had focused on the lips. "Thanks, but it was supposed to be Mick Jagger", she replied.

Lösung

	ENGLISCH		DEUTSCH
1	inspection	=	die Inspektion
2	brave	≠	brav
3	chronological	=	chronologisch
4	accept	=	akzeptieren
5	caricature	=	die Karikatur
	brave	=	tapfer, mutig
	well-behaved, well-mannered	=	**brav**

Richtig wäre:

Most of the children are very **well-mannered** when eating their school dinners. But when the cook tried to serve them raw green tomatoes they threw them around the room.

Try not to lose your appetite whenever you hear about "preservatives" in English food. "Preservative" = "Konservierungsmittel".

A "machine" in English is a piece of equipment or a motor – not usually associated with flying. In our example "Die Maschine" translates as "the aircraft" or "the plane".

16. Personal values

1. More and more people are being attacked because of their religion. Thank God I'm an **atheist**!

2. David has always been subversive. Even at **kindergarten**, he organized the other children to demand healthier puddings for lunch.

3. People tell me that I'm too **religious**. But what can I do? After all, I am a priest.

4. I don't think that wanting a big house, a fast car and luxury holidays makes Anna **materialistic**. Lots of people want those things these days. It's just that she's unusual in wanting those things *and* belonging to the Communist Party.

5. Annabelle is the type of girl who likes to get **engaged**. It's good that she cares so much but I don't think she can continue to run her Eco-friendly Weddings service from her desk at the bank.

Lösung

	ENGLISCH		DEUTSCH
1	atheist	=	der Atheist
2	kindergarten	=	Der Kindergarten
3	religious	=	religiös
4	materialistic	=	materialistisch
5	engaged	≠	engagiert
	engaged	=	verlobt
	involved, committed, dedicated	=	**engagiert**

Richtig wäre:

Annabelle is the type of girl who likes to get **involved**. It's good that she cares so much but I don't think she can continue to run her Eco-friendly Weddings service from her desk at the bank.

17. More news headlines

1. NEW BROADWAY MUSICAL **DEGENERATES** INTO FARCE
   Actor forced to **improvise** when his pants fall down

2. MILITARY LEADER TO END **AUTOCRATIC** RULE
   It's no fun being a **despot**, says Major-General Madman

3. WE ARE NOT **BOURGEOIS**, SAY FILM STAR COUPLE
   Actress launches **tirade** from their "Winter Palace" home

4. MUSEUM BUYS OBSCURE PAINTING BY PICASSO
   Experts unsure which way new **acquisition** should hang

5. SHORTAGE OF **MIST** KEEPS PRICES HIGH
   Horse owners smell a **win** as gardening becomes most popular weekend activity

Lösung

	ENGLISCH		DEUTSCH
1	degenerate improvise	= =	degenerieren, zurückbilden improvisieren
2	autocratic despot	= =	autokratisch, selbstherrlich der Despot
3	bourgeois tirade	= =	der Bourgeois, Kleinbürger die Tirade
4	acquisition	=	die Akquisition Anschaffung, Erwerb
5	mist win	≠ ≠	der Mist der Gewinn
	mist win	= =	leichter Nebel erlangen, gewinnen
	dung **profit**	= =	**der Mist** **der Gewinn**

Richtig wäre:

SHORTAGE OF **DUNG** KEEPS PRICES HIGH

Horse owners smell a **profit** as gardening becomes most popular weekend activity

18. It must be love

1. I tried to look **nonchalant** when lovely Loretta walked into the room. But the effect was lost when I spilled red wine on her new shoes.

2. Nadia is so beautiful but I really can't understand her **accent**. And, sadly, she doesn't seem to understand my body language!

3. Keith said he would swim across a river full of crocodiles if I were on the other side. But I knew that was just **bravado** when I found him hiding from a mouse in the kitchen.

4. When Simon said he would like to "see more of me", I thought it was **romantic** innuendo. I realized I was wrong when after 10 dates he still hadn't tried to kiss me.

5. My sister's boyfriend kept saying she'd look really sexy with short **hairs**. So she cut them, and it was true: she was so much more attractive that she soon got a much nicer boyfriend.

Lösung

	ENGLISCH		DEUTSCH
1	nonchalant	=	nonchalant, (lässig)
2	accent	=	der Akzent
3	bravado	=	das Bravado, (Tapferkeit)
4	romantic	=	romantisch
5	hairs	≠	das Haar
	hairs	=	die Schamhaare
	hair (ohne „s")!	=	**Haar**

Richtig wäre:

My sister's boyfriend kept saying she'd look really sexy with short **hair**. So she cut it, and it was true: she was so much more attractive that she soon got a much nicer boyfriend.

19. Family Trouble

1. My husband is so **egocentric** that even his psychiatrist is tired of hearing him talk about himself.

2. I'm worried that my 16-year-old son is becoming an **introvert**. He's stayed home for two evenings in the past month,and last night he read a book.

3. Five hundred people came to watch my film show on Monday evening but it was a total **disaster**. Instead of photographs of the white whale swimming in the Atlantic, I had accidentally brought pictures of my wife playing in the hotel pool. Yes, she is rather a large lady.

4. Miranda has gone too far with her need for **symmetry**. Last weekend she brought home *two* boyfriends for Sunday lunch. Having one handsome man on her right and another on her left made her feel more comfortable, she said.

5. My father is a very successful **undertaker**, and although Mum likes the money he earns, she doesn't like it when he brings his work home with him.

Lösung

	ENGLISCH		DEUTSCH
1	egocentric	=	egozentrisch, (ich-bezogen)
2	introvert	=	introvertiert
3	disaster	=	das Desaster
4	symmetry	=	die Symmetrie
5	undertaker	≠	der Unternehmer
	undertaker	=	der Leichenbestatter, das Beerdigungsinstitut
	entrepreneur	=	**der Unternehmer**

Richtig wäre:

My father is a very successful **entrepreneur**, and although Mum likes the money he earns, she doesn't like it when he brings his work home with him.

20. It's a man's world

1. My golf club is the last **bastion** of good manners in England. We still open doors for the ladies. (Well, just *one* door really, because they're not allowed in the other rooms.)

2. A magazine this week listed the 100 Top Business People in Britain. The word 'people' was naturally a **euphemism** for 'men'. There wasn't one woman among them!

3. I have asked our optician if she'll **control** my husband's eyes. Since he turned 65, he seems to find every woman under 40 years old extremely attractive.

4. Formula One has always been run by a **cabal** of men. It's hard to imagine that there'll ever be a Bernadette Ecclestone or a Michaela Schumacher.

5. David understands the **concept** of washing machines – he just finds it hard to remember how they work.

Lösung

	ENGLISCH		DEUTSCH
1	bastion	=	die Bastion
2	euphemism	=	der Euphemismus, (Schönfärberei)
3	control	≠	kontrollieren
4	cabal	=	die Kabale, (der Clan)
5	concept	=	das Konzept
	control	=	ansteuern, beherrschen, beeinflussen, führen
	check, examine	=	**kontrollieren**

Richtig wäre:

I have asked our optician if she'll **check** my husband's eyes. Since he turned 65, he seems to find every woman under 40 years old extremely attractive.

Oh dear! The addition of a single "s" to the word "hair" changes its meaning to "Schamhaar". Don't pluralise this word unless you really mean it, i.e. in a hotel "Call the manager. There are hairs in the bed!"

Only the very rich can afford their own private cook. Don't confuse the German "Chef" with the French-English "chef" or the slang "chief". Simply talk about your "boss".

21. The difficulties of parenting

1. My wife thinks I'm very **reactionary** but I simply don't believe that allowing one's children to grow hashish in the kitchen is a sign of great progress in society.

2. I used to boast that I had endless **reserves** of energy but now that I have three children I don't have the strength to defend that statement.

3. I had to disagree with Judy when she described kids as being "like **parasites**". I pointed out that fleas and mosquitoes were actually much easier to shake off.

4. Choosing the best time to talk about sex with one's children is a **sensible** matter. But we obviously waited far too long to speak to our son because when I asked if he knew about safe sex, he replied: "Yes, what do you need to know?"

5. Our children are only five and six but they already seem like **miniature** adults. I don't know how that's happened because my husband and I still behave like big kids.

Lösung

	ENGLISCH		DEUTSCH
1	reactionary	=	reaktionär
2	reserves	=	die Reserven
3	parasites	=	die Parasiten
4	sensible	≠	sensibel
5	miniature	=	Miniatur
	sensible	=	vernünftig
	sensitive	=	**sensibel**

Richtig wäre:

Choosing the best time to talk about sex with one's children is a **sensitive** matter. But we obviously waited far too long to speak to our son because when I asked if he knew about safe sex, he replied: "Yes, what do you need to know?"

22. An easy mistake to make

1. I asked Mr Jacobs where he got his **energy** from. "I eat bananas for breakfast, make love to my wife regularly and go to the toilet at the same time every day," he replied. He was a little embarrassed when I said that I actually wanted to know which company supplied his electricity.

2. My work as an undercover detective means I have to be **anonymous** sometimes. My girlfriend says that's why she sometimes whispers another man's name when we're in bed. Should I believe her?

3. Mr Hooper was about to raise a glass of Champagne **on the ladies** when someone told him there were no women in the room. The young men at the O'Murphy School of Art all had such long hair in the 1970s, you see.

4. During my interview, I was told that the company **hierarchy** was more or less "flat". I thought this meant that everyone was equal, but now I realize it means that most of the directors have to lie down after lunch.

5. It's difficult to **assimilate** a lot of new information in a short period of time. I think that's why I sent my boss to a conference in Paris, Texas, instead of Paris, France. He was so angry, he refused to bring me a cowboy hat back.

Lösung

	ENGLISCH		DEUTSCH
1	energy	=	die Energie
2	anonymous	=	anonym
3	on the ladies	≠	auf die Damen!
4	hierarchy	=	die Hierarchie
5	assimilate	=	assimilieren (hier: aufnehmen)
	on the ladies	=	Springt auf die Damen!
	to the ladies	=	**auf die Damen!**

Richtig wäre:

Mr Hooper was about to raise a glass of Champagne **to the ladies** when someone told him there were no women in the room. The young men at the O'Murphy School of Art all had such long hair in the 1970s, you see.

23. Business News

1. FINANCIAL **CRISIS** AT TOP MUNICH FIRM
   CEO offers resignation after leaving secret papers in Oktoberfest beer hall

2. MUSIC INDUSTRY 'MUST NOT **DISCRIMINATE** AGAINST OLD PEOPLE'
   I can still sing and be **decadent**, 84-year-old rocker tells studio bosses. It's only the dancing that hurts.

3. INTERNET COMPANY JUST A CLICK AWAY FROM **INSOLVENCY**
   Plans for **amortization** to be announced today

4. BANANA GROWERS **TRANSFER** PRODUCTION TO UK
   Climate change makes Scotland perfect for oranges, too

5. BASEL GIRLS GET BIG BREASTS WITH SMALL **CAUTION**
   Swiss clinic lets poorer women to pay for silicon in monthly **rates**.

Lösung

	ENGLISCH		DEUTSCH
1	crisis	=	die Krise
	discriminate	=	diskriminieren
2	decadent	=	dekadent, entartet
	insolvency	=	die Insolvenz
3	amortization	=	die Amortisation, Tilgung
	transfer	=	der Transfer
4	climate	=	das Klima
	caution	≠	die Kaution
5	rates	≠	die Raten
	caution	=	die Vorsicht
	rates	=	die Grundsteuer (UK)
	deposit, security, surety, down-payment	=	**die Kaution (Anzahlung)**
	instalments	=	**die Raten**

Richtig wäre:

BASEL GIRLS GET BIG BREASTS WITH SMALL **DEPOSIT**
Swiss clinic lets poorer women to pay for silicon in monthly **instalments**.

24. Too good to be true

1. The man I met on the Internet told me he didn't work but had a regular income. I thought he was a young stud from a wealthy family but I just found out he's 74 years old and lives on his **rent**.

2. I like Nadia because she is **harmless**. But I'll love her even more when she's not!

3. *First guy:* I have so much respect for Emily. She has the most wonderful brain. Did I tell you she's an **prominent** linguistics professor at Birmingham University?
   Second guy: Yes, you also said she had the longest legs, blondest hair and prettiest smile in Britain.
   First guy: Well, there are those things, too!

4. There's nothing I would change about Henry. He's intelligent, funny, kind, tall and comes from a very **aristocratic** family. Oh, and I nearly forgot to say, he is rather rich.

5. *First girl:* "My new boyfriend is an **absolute** angel!"
   Second girl: "Really? What's his name?"
   First Girl: "Gabriel."

Lösung

	ENGLISCH		DEUTSCH
1	rent	≠	die Rente
2	harmless	=	harmlos, unschuldig
3	prominent	=	prominent
4	aristocratic	=	aristokratisch
5	absolute	=	absolut
	rent	=	die Miete
	die Rente	=	**pension**

Richtig wäre:

The man I met on the Internet told me he didn't work but had a regular income. I thought he was a young stud from a wealthy family but I just found out he's 74 years old and lives on his **pension**.

25. Nobody said it would be like this ...

1. I told Eric that I didn't feel pretty anymore. "That's **humbug**!" he said. But then he added: "Anyway, you've still got a super personality." It wasn't exactly the answer I was hoping for!

2. Married life is not as **idyllic** as I thought it would be. We used to spend weekends in Biarritz and Barcelona - now his idea of a perfect Sunday is me watching him play cricket.

3. It took me 12 university years to get my **promotion** and now I'm working for Shophaus - as a cleaner.

4. *First woman:* "I hate it when Bobby uses the 'F' word.
   Second woman: "But I can't believe your Bobby would use such language."
   First woman: "Well, he does. Just last night he said: 'Kitty, we've got to be **frugal** for a few months'. And he knows how upset I get when I can't shop at Bloomingdales."

5. Divorce can be such a **trauma** for both people. And it's so expensive, too. Fred and I have decided to stay together: that way, we get the unhappiness but at least we're not paying for it.

Lösung

	ENGLISCH		DEUTSCH
1	humbug	=	der Humbug
2	idyllic	=	idyllisch
3	promotion	≠	promovieren
4	frugal	=	frugal, (genügsam, schlicht, einfach)
5	trauma	=	das Trauma
	promotion	=	die Beförderung, die Berufsförderung
	graduate	=	**promovieren**

Richtig wäre:

It took me 12 university years to **graduate** and now I'm working for Shophaus - as a cleaner.

A small but very consequential error. To avoid the suggestion of an orgy (at least during formal occasions) prefer the preposition "to" when toasting. Correct = "To the ladies!"

Don't mix up "Landschaft" with "landscape" which in English is the domain of museums and old masters. It's safer (and nicer) to drive through the "countryside".

26. Excuses, excuses

1. Darren said he couldn't finish the report because a giant bird flew through his window and stole the computer.
It's not exactly a **plausible** story, is it?

2. Jill says she has to work late every evening or she won't get a **bonus** at Christmas. Personally, I think the handsome night porter is the 'extra' that she's hoping for.

3. Little Lenny said he got a disappointing **note** for his music examination because a bad cold had affected his hearing. Do you think Beethoven's mother had to listen to excuses like this?

4. Marsha's lecture on Thursday is sure to be another anticapitalist **polemic**. How can I tell her I'd rather go to the party over at Citibank?

5. I wish Antonio wouldn't **degrade** himself by continually inviting Jemima to dinner. Does he really believe she's been 'busy' every night for the past eight weeks?

Lösung

	ENGLISCH		DEUTSCH
1	plausible	=	plausibel
2	bonus	=	der Bonus
3	note	≠	die (Prüfungs-) Note
4	polemic	=	die Polemik
5	degrade	=	degradieren
	note	=	Briefchen, Aktennotiz
	mark, grade	=	**die (Prüfungs-) Note**

Richtig wäre:

Little Lenny said he got a disappointing **mark** for his music examination because a bad cold had affected his hearing. Do you think Beethoven's mother had to listen to excuses like this?

27. Wild times

1. Don't tell me that my fear of spiders isn't **rational**! Not until *you've* woken up and found a tarantula in your pyjamas.

2. My father had an **aversion** to horses all his life. That makes things really difficult when you're a cowboy.

3. Colin always had a love_of_snakes. It was just so **tragic** that the boa constrictor he met in the forest didn't feel the same about him.

4. I had read 60 pages of Franz Kafka's **Metamorphosis** before I realized it wouldn't help me with my college project on the lifecycle of insects.

5. Mother told us never to play in the **barracks** in Mr Cooper's field. She said three tigers lived inside but when we got older we discovered the true reason: the walls were covered in 'naughty' pictures from magazines. We played there a lot after that!

Lösung

	ENGLISCH		DEUTSCH
1	rational	=	rational
2	aversion	=	die Aversion
3	tragic	=	tragisch
4	metamorphosis	=	die Metamorphose, (Verwandlung)
5	barracks	≠	die Baracke
	barracks	=	die Kaserne
	hut, shack	=	**die Baracke**

Richtig wäre:

Mother told us never to play in the **huts** in Mr Cooper's field. She said three tigers lived inside but when we got older we discovered the true reason: the walls were covered in 'naughty' pictures from magazines. We played there a lot after that!

28. Language problems ... and solutions

1. Basic English is easy to learn; it's the **idiomatic** expressions that cause problems, by and large. See what I mean?

2. I tried to **consolidate** all the English I'd learned at school by taking a trip to Wales so that I could actually *use* it. No one told me I'd chosen a village where they speak only Welsh!

3. Learning English is a struggle but I won't let its vocabulary **besiege** me. It may have 500,000 words but many are borrowed from German - and when I hear English people mispronounce Doppelgänger I feel a little Schadenfreude.

4. Do you want to know a secret? People think I'm fluent in English but it's just an **illusion**. Most of my vocabulary comes from Beatles lyrics, and if a word isn't in one of their songs, I think Help!

5. I find the language books published by Daniel & Co a little too **didactic**. I prefer to have fun while I'm learning, which is why I chose this book!

Lösung

	ENGLISCH		DEUTSCH
1	idiomatic	=	idiomatisch
2	consolidate	=	konsolidieren, festigen
3	besiege	≠	besiegen
4	illusion	=	die Illusion
5	didactic	=	didaktisch
	besiege	=	bedrängen, belagern, überhäufen, umlagern
	to beat, to conquer, to defeat, to lick [coll.], to outgun so., to out-play, to overwhelm, to subdue, to vanquish, to walk over s.o.	=	**besiegen**

Richtig wäre:

Learning English is a struggle but I won't let its vocabulary **beat** me. It may have 500,000 words but many are borrowed from German – and when I hear English people mispronounce Doppelgänger I feel a little Schadenfreude.

29. Cultural matters

1. Mike's private collection covers the whole **spectrum** of 20th-century art. Sadly, the range of talent is rather narrower, going from bad to very bad.

2. At our evening class last night, the tutor told us that Moby Dick had been interpreted as an **allegory** about life, death, religion, American society and lots of other things.
   Why aren't my fishing trips that interesting to people?

3. The theatre critic used such **esoteric** language that it was difficult to understand his article, let alone disagree with it.

4. The political **dissident** was delighted to be invited to speak at the party conference. He was less pleased when they told him that he would not be allowed to enter the country until three days after the event had ended.

5. While on holiday in Cape Town we bought a painting by an **Afrikaner** called Robert Mumbumbi. It shows a group of antelope looking at a microwave oven. I've no idea what it means but I like the colours.

Lösung

	ENGLISCH		DEUTSCH
1	spectrum	=	das Spektrum
2	allegory	=	die Allegorie (das Gleichnis)
3	esoteric	=	esoterisch
4	dissident	=	der Dissident
5	Afrikaner	≠	der Afrikaner
	Afrikaner	=	der Bure (ein Weißer)
	(black) African	=	**der Afrikaner**

Richtig wäre:

While on holiday in Cape Town we bought a painting by an **black African** called Robert Mumbumbi. It shows a group of antelope looking at a microwave oven. I've no idea what it means but I like the colours.

30. Very (very) important people?

1. The Princess of Devon has launched an **inquisition** to find out who put 12 mm of toothpaste on her toothbrush yesterday morning. Everyone at the palace knows she likes to have 14 mm.

2. I don't think it's **ethical** for the same person to be chairman and chief executive. But our chairman says it is his duty to appoint the best person to manage the company, and that he IS the best person.

3. If Lady Lockhampton would kindly **communicate** with me *personally*, I'd be able to tell her that she has won the Lottery.

4. Lord Loopy had to cancel his visit to Buckingham Palace for '**familiar** reasons'. I heard later that it was because his favourite goldfish was sick.

5. Sir Henry arrived back from his stay at Maison Mirabelle with a **litany** of complaints. Why, he asked, was there no toy duck for his bathtub? And since when did hotels stop providing silk pillows?

Lösung

	ENGLISCH		DEUTSCH
1	inquisition	=	die Inquisition, gerichtliche Untersuchung
2	ethical	=	ethisch, moralisch
3	communicate	=	kommunizieren
4	familiar	≠	familiär
5	litany	=	die Litanei
	familiar	=	bekannt, geläufig, vertraut
	family or familial	=	**familiär**

Richtig wäre:

Lord Loopy had to cancel his visit to Buckingham Palace for '**family** reasons'. I heard later that it was because his favourite goldfish was sick.

Don't be shocked if your English-speaking colleague says he's "hot" - this is not necessarily the start of an amorous adventure. I am hot = "mir ist heiß".

An old mistake, but all too often heard. "Bekommen" is not "become" (= werden), but "get". In better restaurants prefer to say "I would like … (the pork)".

31. False impressions

1. I was upset to discover that my Tai Chi teacher was a total **charlatan**. Everything he knew, he'd learned from watching people in a park in Stuttgart.

2. Scientific **analysis** showed that the unusual 'silver' wedding rings we bought in Peru were, in fact, made from Coca-Cola cans.

3. It was only *after* the expensive **abstract** painting arrived at our home, that we realized it was not by an artist called Lily Agedfour. It was by Lily, Aged Four.

4. Franc liked to think he knew everything about classical music. But when he said Edward Elgar was Norway's greatest composer, I knew he was just a **dilettante**.

5. We thought our daughter's new baby-sitter looked like a **serious** girl but when she stole our antique silver spoons we realized that the fact she wore glasses was probably not a good basis for our judgement.

Lösung

	ENGLISCH		DEUTSCH
1	charlatan	=	der Scharlatan
2	analysis	=	die Analyse
3	abstract	=	abstrakt
4	dilettante	=	der Dilettant
5	serious	≠	seriös
	serious	=	ernst
	reliable, respectable, honest	=	**seriös**

Richtig wäre:

We thought our daughter's new baby-sitter looked like a **reliable** girl but when she stole our antique silver spoons we realized that the fact she wore glasses was probably not a good basis for our judgment.

32. So, why did you quit that job (honestly)?

1. "I got tired of all the negative comments from my boss. Constructive **criticism** is OK, but when he said I was 'as much use as a chocolate sun hat,' I got really upset."

2. "After *that* **scandal**, do you really think I had a choice? But I promise it won't happen again. I'm happily married now.

3. "Oh, that place was way too **conventional** for me. If I want to wear a Hawaiian shirt with my suit, I think I should be allowed to. And I'm sure other senior members of the Pentagon staff feel the same."

4. "It was a mistake for me to become an accountant. I really enjoyed maths at **gymnasium** - but then I also loved my acting classes and no one suggested I should become a politician."

5. "The National Association of Journalists called a one-day **strike** over pay. Unfortunately, I got the day wrong. The editor said that reporters who couldn't get their facts right, shouldn't be on his staff."

Lösung

	ENGLISCH		DEUTSCH
1	criticism	=	die Kritik
2	scandal	=	der Skandal
3	conventional	=	konventionell
4	gymnasium	≠	das Gymnasium
5	strike	=	der Streik
	gymnasium	=	die Turnhalle
	high school (US) **grammar school (Brit.)**	=	**das Gymnasium**

Richtig wäre:

"It was a mistake for me to become an accountant. I really enjoyed maths at **grammar school** - but then I also loved my acting classes and no one suggested I should become a politician."

33. Planes, trains and autobahns

1. A senior politician was sitting next to me on the flight to San Diego. He watched the cartoon **channel** for the whole journey, which was rather worrying.

2. I said "**Good Appetite**" to my English friends before we ate dinner at a motorway cafe but they didn't say anything back. Once I tasted the food, I realised I should have said "Good Luck!".

3. Our train was delayed 12 hours when the police found a passenger carrying illegal cigarettes. By midnight, we were begging the officers to give us some of the **contraband** to keep us calm – but they said smoking onboard wasn't allowed.

4. The **labyrinth** of roads around Potsville is so confusing that the authorities are giving prizes to drivers who reach the middle of the city without getting lost on the way.

5. We were riding through the Blue Ridge Mountains in complete **harmony** with nature when suddenly we arrived at an "All You Can Eat for $2.99" burger bar.

Lösung

	ENGLISCH		DEUTSCH
1	channel	=	der Kanal, (hier: TV-Kanal)
2	Good Appetite	≠	Guten Appetit!
3	contraband	=	die Kontrabande, (Schmuggelware)
4	labyrinth	=	das Labyrinth
5	harmony	=	die Harmonie
	Good Appetite	=	großer Hunger (!)
	Enjoy your meal!* bon appetit!	=	**Guten Appetit!**

* often nothing is said in the US & UK before starting to eat – just wait for the host(ess) to begin, or to signal that you can start.

Richtig wäre:

I said "**Enjoy your meal**" to my English friends before we ate dinner at a motorway cafe but they didn't say anything back. Once I tasted the food, I realised I should have said "Good Luck!".

34. News in Brief

1. Did you know that the world spent more than a **billion** dollars shopping on the Internet in 2002 - up from $600,000,000,000 in 2001? Guess that's what you call a shop.com revolution!

2. World-famous **astrologer** Charlotte-Ann Trix had to cancel her séance at the National Hall last night due to unforeseen circumstances.

3. A **corrupt** bank manager who stole nearly $1 million from his customers told police that he wanted "a movie star lifestyle". Miramont Pictures have now announced they are to make a film about the man's life.

4. The Victoria Library has announced an **amnesty** next week for people who have not returned their books. One valuable item that has been missing for 17 years is a novel called "Honesty".

5. Billco Supermarket is refusing to **compensate** a customer who claims that the avocados she bought did not become ripe in time for her dinner party. The woman wants £10,000 for the damage caused to her social life.

Lösung

	ENGLISCH		DEUTSCH
1	billion	≠	die Billion
2	astrologer	=	Astrologe
3	corrupt	=	korrupt
4	amnesty	=	die Amnestie
5	compensate	=	kompensieren, (hier: entschuldigen)
	billion	=	die Milliarde
	trillion	=	**Billion**

Richtig wäre:

Did you know that the world spent more than a **trillion** dollars shopping on the Internet in 2002 - up from $600,000,000,000 in 2001? Guess that's what you call a shop.com revolution!

35. What can I get for you?

1. We'd like four bottles of the Sancerre. And it would be **correct** for us to order a bottle of Coke for our young guests, too.

2. I'd like a **bloody** steak with carrots, beans and two baked potatoes … as my starter.

3. We can't decide. Is there a **special** dish that you can recommend?

4. Just a mixed salad, please. My trainer has given me a **rigorous** fitness program that doesn't allow me to eat any fat.

5. I'd like the salmon but I need you to serve the Hollandaise sauce on a separate plate. That's just my little **idiosyncrasy**.

Lösung

	ENGLISCH		DEUTSCH
1	correct	=	korrekt
2	bloody	≠	blutig
3	special	=	speziell
4	rigorous	=	rigoros
5	idiosyncrasy	=	die Idiosynkrasie (die Eigenart, Eigenheit)
	bloody	=	verdammt, blöd
	rare	=	**blutig**

Richtig wäre:

I'd like a **rare** steak with carrots, beans and two baked potatoes … as my starter.

Unfortunately the German "fahrt" is indistiguishable from the English "fart" (furzen). It's more polite to wish your guest a "good trip" or a "safe trip" instead.

How many millions of man-hours could be saved by realising that the English "half-nine" is "halb zehn" a full hour later than the German "halb neun". Simply say "eight-thirty".

36. Simple explanations

1. Tony couldn't **diagnose** the fault with my printer. So, he kicked it. That worked!

2. Kevin seemed strangely **reserved** about being interviewed on TV yesterday afternoon. Then I realized he'd somehow got lipstick on his shirt during lunch.

3. Maurice sent me an email saying he'd fallen in love with a goat in the South of France. I had some sleepless nights until he explained he meant to type 'boat'. What a difference one **consonant** can make!

4. I couldn't understand why my partner reacted so badly when I called to tell him I was having his baby. I was about to cry but then I realized that I'd dialed a **false number**.

5. When I first saw Anna, she was talking to my husband and **gesticulating** wildly. I thought she must be angry. But she's just Italian!

Lösung

	ENGLISCH		DEUTSCH
1	diagnose	=	diagnostizieren
2	reserved	=	reserviert
3	consonant	=	der Konsonant
4	false number	≠	falsche Nummer
5	gesticulate	=	gestikulieren
	false number	=	nicht wahre, nicht echte Nummer
	wrong number	=	**falsche Nummer**

Richtig wäre:

I couldn't understand why my partner reacted so badly when I called to tell him I was having his baby. I was about to cry but then I realized that I'd dialed a **wrong number**.

37. Food for thought

1. The chocolate pudding at Mr Joe's tastes **exquisite**. But you know what they say: "A minute on the tongue, a lifetime on the hips!"

2. "I don't know which restaurant to choose for the Christmas dinner," said my new secretary. "The Sushi Bar is excellent but quite expensive. The Steak House is cheap but a long way away. I'm sure you can understand my **dilemma**." "Not really," I said. "I'm a vegetarian."

3. Every year, Aunt Hildegard made me a **biscuit** for my birthday. It was big enough to share with at least 10 friends but as no other kids lived in Hameln, I had to eat it all.

4. The guidebook described La Grotto as a **cosmopolitan** restaurant, so I was surprised to find only burgers and sandwiches on the menu. When I complained, the waiter told me to f*** o**. But, I must admit, he did say it in seven languages.

5. Our cook has served sausages and chips for lunch every day this week. I don't mind so much, but my dog says a little **innovation** would be very welcome with him!

Lösung

	ENGLISCH		DEUTSCH
1	exquisite	=	exquisit
2	dilemma	=	das Dilemma
3	biscuit	≠	Biskuit
4	cosmopolitan	=	kosmopolitisch, weltoffen
5	innovation	=	die Innovation
	biscuit (UK) biscuit (US)	= =	der Keks, das Plätzchen kleines, festes Brötchen
	sponge cake	=	**Biskuit**

Richtig wäre:

Every year, Aunt Clara made me a **sponge cake** for my birthday. It was big enough to share with at least 10 friends but as no other kids lived in Hameln, I had to eat it all.

38. At the conference centre

1. We thought it would be best to make only a **nominal** charge for the "How to Save Money" seminar.

2. The speaker at last year's conference on sleeping problems had such a **monotonous** voice that we all found it difficult to stay awake.

3. At next month's training course there will be **parallel** workshops on decision-making and time-management. But I can't decide which would be the best use of my time.

4. Organizers of the Japanese Bonsai exhibition say the **echo** to invitations has been much smaller than expected.

5. The bar staff at the Caton Center only get paid **provisions**. So it was a bad week when Alcoholics Anonymous and the Abstinence Society held their meetings there at the same time.

Lösung

	ENGLISCH		DEUTSCH
1	nominal	=	nominal
2	monotonous	=	monoton
3	parallel	=	parallel
4	echo	=	das Echo
5	provisions	≠	die Provision
	provisions	=	die Bestimmungen, die Rückstellungen, die Maßnahmen, die Lebensmittel, der Proviant
	commission	=	**die Provision**

Richtig wäre:

The bar staff at the Caton Center only get paid **commission**. So it was a bad week when Alcoholics Anonymous and the Abstinence Society held their meetings there at the same time.

39. Hospital chief executive talks to his staff

1. I have called you here today to remind you that all staff must be **precise** in matters of hygiene …

2. … Nurses, especially, are asked to ensure that all medical instruments are **sterile** before patients are prepared for surgery …

3. Last week, Dr Johnstone faced a difficult **situation** when he saw that the knife he was going to use in an operation had something red on it …

4. … Naturally, he thought it was blood, although it was, in fact, ketchup from someone's lunch. **When** he hadn't been so observant …

5. … This mistake could have caused **acute** embarrassment for my hospital. Sorry, I mean acute suffering to the patient.

Lösung

	ENGLISCH		DEUTSCH
1	precise	=	präzise
2	sterile	=	steril
3	situation	=	die Situation
4	when	≠	wenn (falls)
5	acute	=	akut
	when	=	als, wann, sobald
	if*	=	**wenn**

* Use "If" with conditionals I, II, & III, not "when"

Richtig wäre:

… Naturally, he thought it was blood, although it was, in fact, ketchup from someone's lunch. **If** he hadn't been so observant …

40. War and Peace

1. The toy soldiers' **offensive** on Teddy Bear Mountain might have been more successful if they hadn't used plastic guns.

2. When the enemy appeared on the **horizon**, I told my men to move forward … so that I could hide behind them.

3. "I think war is **morally** wrong," said Glenda. "And I'd fight anyone who challenged that belief."

4. I hope this country won't go to war before the end of the year. My boyfriend is in the army and I **will** him home to make Christmas dinner.

5. Helmuth von Moltke said: "No plan survives contact with the enemy." It is therefore my **hypothesis** that the best plan would be to avoid ever meeting an enemy.

Lösung

	ENGLISCH		DEUTSCH
1	offensive	=	die Offensive
2	horizon	=	der Horizont
3	morally	=	moralisch
4	will	≠	wollen
5	hypothesis	=	die Hypothese
	will	=	werden
	want, would like	=	**wollen**

Richtig wäre:

I hope this country won't go to war before the end of the year. My boyfriend is in the army and I **want** him home to make Christmas dinner.

Remember that any suggestion of "private parts" (particularly between the sexes) is associated more with bodies than with buildings! To avoid confusion just show your guest "the house".

An unfortunate co-incidence that "Fliege" and "fly" refer to different parts of a man's costume. Ladies (and men) should better say "Nice bow-tie", at least in public!

41. Teenage Troubles

1. Michael is becoming increasingly **insolent**. When I suggested to him that he was mixing with bad people, he said: "Yes, you and Dad."

2. First teenager: "I don't think Andy and I are **compatible**."
   Second teenager: "You must be joking! I thought you two were so in love."
   First teenager: "So did I. But he's started wearing Adidas trainers and I wear Nike. Big differences like this are important."

3. I'm worried about Matthew. He only got a 'D' for biology, an 'E' for history, although he did get a 'B' for French. I'm sure he has some **latent** talent but he certainly keeps it well hidden most of the time.

4. Terry has started **spending** blood regularly at the hospital. At first I thought he wanted to help people but now I think he's in love with one of the nurses. If he continues like this, his arm will soon be empty!

5. Jamie said she thought Aunt Hilda's new shoes were "unusually attractive". I think she was being **ironic**.

Lösung

	ENGLISCH		DEUTSCH
1	insolent	=	insolent, (anmaßend, unverschämt)
2	compatible	=	kompatibel
3	latent	=	latent, (hier: verborgen)
4	spend	≠	spenden
5	ironic	=	ironisch
	spend	=	Geld ausgeben
	donate	=	**spenden**

Richtig wäre:

Terry has started **donating** blood regularly at the hospital. At first I thought he wanted to help people but now I think he's in love with one of the nurses. If he continues like this, his arm will soon be empty!

42. The weather this week

1. **Sporadic** rain will affect most of Wales on Monday… and the rest of Wales on Tuesday.

2. Following several days of almost tropical sunshine, Cornwall can expect fairly **consequent** snow showers over the next few weeks. So, out go the ice creams, on come the ice skates!

3. Central England will be cold but sunny for the first half of the week, and warm but cloudy for the second. Weather can be so **illogical** sometimes.

4. After eight days of rain, the sun will **compensate** the people of eastern Scotland tomorrow by making theirs the hottest region in the UK. (Wet weather returns on Friday.)

5. Strong winds will blow across Northern Ireland on Monday and Tuesday. It might be **wise** for women not to wear skirts.

Lösung

	ENGLISCH		DEUTSCH
1	sporadic	=	sporadisch
2	consequent	≠	konsequent
3	illogical	=	unlogisch
4	compensate	=	kompensieren, (hier:Ausgleich schaffen für)
5	wise	=	weise, klug; angebracht
	consequent	=	folgend
	consistent	=	**konsequent**

Richtig wäre:

Following several days of almost tropical sunshine, Cornwall can expect fairly **consistent** snow showers over the next few weeks. So, out go the ice creams, on come the ice skates!

43. It makes you think

1. When I asked my teacher if he'd **prove** my essay on Existentialism he said only I could be responsible for my own work.

2. I could try to be more **optimistic** but I'm sure that I would fail.

3. Although English has a very large vocabulary, my teacher couldn't think of another word for **synonym**.

4. Co-workers asked me what I thought about my **mentor** leaving the company. I said that I didn't know *what* to think any more.

5. The librarian told me that there was a long waiting list for the new **anthology** of short stories.

Lösung

	ENGLISCH		DEUTSCH
1	prove	≠	prüfen
2	optimistic	=	optimistisch
3	synonym	=	das Synonym
4	mentor	=	der Mentor
5	anthology	=	die Anthologie, (der Sammelband)
	prove	=	beweisen
	check	=	**prüfen**

Richtig wäre:

When I asked my teacher if he'd **check** my essay on Existentialism he said only I could be responsible for my own work.

44. You are what you wear

1. David Beckham is the most **elegant** footballer. Well, can you think of another who looks that good in a sari?

2. Mum likes to **plunder** my wardrobe when she's going out for the evening. She says my clothes are "cool". I can't believe she still cares what is trendy - not now that she's reached 80!

3. I read in a magazine that **horizontal** stripes make you look fat. Shouldn't zebras be told this? Maybe they'd look like gazelles if they dressed in plain black.

4. My new assistant has a rather **idiosyncratic** way of dressing. I think we'll have to keep her away from customers on the days when she wears that Abba outfit.

5. A **probe** involving 5,000 people aged 18 to 48 has found that designer clothes don't make a person more successful in love. Scientists say those who dress at expensive shops have much shorter relationships - perhaps because they fear being seen with last season's partner.

Lösung

	ENGLISCH		DEUTSCH
1	elegant	=	elegant
2	plunder	=	plündern
3	horizontal	=	horizontal
4	idiosyncratic	=	idiosynkratisch, (eigenwillig)
5	probe	≠	die Probe
	probe	=	der Forschungssatellit, die Sonde, die (polizeiliche) Untersuchung
	a survey, a study	=	**die Probe**

Richtig wäre:

A **survey** involving 5,000 people aged 18 to 48 has found that designer clothes don't make a person more successful in love. Scientists say those who dress at expensive shops have much shorter relationships - perhaps because they fear being seen with last season's partner.

45. Older ... but not wiser

1. My eight-year-old daughter asked me what the **superlative** of 'bad' was. I told her I was the worst person in the world at grammar, and that she should ask her mother.

2. As a boy, I could play guitar and knew the names of all the dinosaurs. Now I remember only three **accords** and two dinosaurs - Tyrannosaurus and Brontosaurus. So wouldn't it be better if schools taught just one thing: how not to forget!

3. "Rick," I said, "you've been married nine times, so you must know *everything* about women."
   "Everything except how to keep one," he replied, **laconically**.

4. When David said he wanted to take me to "an **intimate** little place", I should have guessed he meant his bedroom.

5. I asked Mr Williams if he ever went shopping on the Internet. "Oh no," he said, looking at me **consternated**. "I always go on the bus."

Lösung

	ENGLISCH		DEUTSCH
1	superlative	=	die Superlative
2	accord	≠	der Akkord
3	laconically	=	lakonisch
4	intimate	=	intim
5	consternated	=	konsterniert
	accord	=	das Abkommen, die Abmachung
	chord	=	**der Akkord**

Richtig wäre:

As a boy, I could play guitar and knew the names of all the dinosaurs. Now I remember only three **chords** and two dinosaurs – Tyrannosaurus and Brontosaurus. So wouldn't it be better if schools taught just one thing: how not to forget!

46. International News

1. MONACO UNIVERSITY OFFERS NEW DEGREE IN **HEDONISM**
   Elite students to learn about champagne, casinos and fast cars.

2. **DEMOGRAPHIC** CHANGE LEAVES 10 COUNTRIES SHORT OF WOMEN
   Men ordered to disperse (and dress better) to find wives.

3. MUNICH HAS ENERGY-**EFFICIENT** ANSWER TO WINTER HEATING PROBLEM Other states **dubious** as Bavarians burn old lederhosen.

4. ISLANDERS UNHAPPY WITH 'CRAZY' NEW **REGIME**
   Junta loses popularity after trying to sell the sea.

5. WORLD'S LONGEST **PROCESS** ENDS IN DUTCH COURT
   Marmalade company cleared of using unripe strawberries.

Lösung

	ENGLISCH		DEUTSCH
	hedonism	=	der Hedonismus, Genusssucht
1	elite	=	die Elite
2	demographic	=	demographisch
	efficient	=	effizient
3	dubious	=	dubios
	regime	=	das Regime
4	Junta	=	die Junta
	process	≠	Prozess (jur.)
5	marmalade	≠	die Marmelade
	process	=	der Ablauf, der Arbeitsvorgang;
	Marmalade	=	die Orangenmarmelade
	court case, legal action	=	**Prozess** (jur.)
	jam	=	**die Marmelade**

Richtig wäre:

World's longest **court case** ends in Dutch court, **jam** company cleared of using unripe strawberries.

Say the word "fax" out loud – if it rhymes with "ducks" then take care. Your mind is OK but your mouth is saying "fucks"!!! Avoid this pronunciation at work, or use email instead.

"Must not" = "darf nicht" and is a most dangerous translation mistake. Germans wanting to be polite, sound arrogant. Be sure to use the phrase "Don't have to ..."

Quiz

47. For sale

1. We are pleased to offer this **classic** English cottage in a beautiful part of Oxfordshire. Two bedrooms, good-sized kitchen and rose garden. All that's missing is … the roof!

2. Do you like having lots of visitors? Do you enjoy **nostalgia**? Then we have the perfect house for you – right here in Memphis! Built in 1939, with eight bedrooms, four bathrooms, and a Jungle Room. Previous owner possibly still living there!

3. Large five-bedroom apartment in one of London's most **opulent** neighbourhoods. Parking for three Aston Martins.

4. Come to Cardinal Village, an **oasis** of peace right in the middle of Atlanta! Here you'll find 24 family villas, each with beautiful gardens and swimming pool. You can almost hear the birds sing (of course, you really *could* hear them sing until we started building these houses).

5. Be the first to see the latest fashions and furniture arrive! This luxurious town house opposite Hamburg's most famous **warehouse** is perfect for people who like a busy scene right outside their window.

Lösung

	ENGLISCH		DEUTSCH
1	classic	=	klassisch
2	nostalgia	=	die Nostalgie
3	opulent	=	opulent, (hier auch: reich)
4	oasis	=	die Oase
5	warehouse	≠	das Warenhaus
	warehouse	=	das Warenlager, die Lagerhalle
	department store	=	**das Warenhaus**

Richtig wäre:

Be the first to see the latest fashions and furniture arrive! This luxurious town house opposite Hamburg's most famous **department store** is perfect for people who like a busy scene right outside their window.

48. Designs for Living

1. Ted has chosen a **heterogeneous** mix of styles for his new home. His bedroom, for example, has Bauhaus furniture and Barbie Doll curtains.

2. Our chairman wanted a wildlife **motif** to run throughout the new office designs. It's OK having a picture of a tiger in the reception, but having a snake on the toilet seats makes me rather nervous.

3. This building was not **renovated** when the company bought it two years ago - but that didn't stop us moving in. On rainy days, we sat at our desks with umbrellas over our heads.

4. The new villa has everything we want - except the **infrastructure** to reach it. The nearest road ends 2 km away, so we have to travel the last part by camel.

5. I asked a property expert to value my new architect designed home. I was surprised when she said it was worth only £900,000. "I want to get another **meaning**," I told her. "OK," she replied, "I think your dog is really ugly."

Lösung

	ENGLISCH		DEUTSCH
1	heterogeneous	=	heterogen, (verschiedenartig)
2	motif	=	das Motiv
3	renovate	=	renovieren
4	infrastructure	=	die Infrastruktur
5	meaning	≠	die Meinung
	meaning	=	die Bedeutung
	opinion	=	**Meinung**

Richtig wäre:

I asked a property expert to value my new architect designed home. I was surprised when she said it was worth only £ 900,000. "I want to get another **opinion**," I told her. "OK," she replied, "I think your dog is really ugly."

49. The (difficult) art of small talk

1. When Liza gave a **subtle** cough, Max knew he'd told their guests more than enough about the sex life of African frogs.

2. Sidney never knew what to say to people at parties. But tonight his **authentic** Mongolian horse-riding trousers got everyone talking.

3. The conversation at our company's Christmas dinner is usually so **banal**. This year, I'm going to make sure we discuss interesting things, such as military history. I'm sure everyone will be grateful.

4. Before my son's first visit to an expensive restaurant, I gave him a tip: if you can't think what to say, talk about something on the **card**. Imagine his girlfriend's face when he said: "Did you see the dead fly on the Entrees page?"

5. At social events, I never talk about sex, politics or religion. They're too **controversial**. Health is a much more suitable subject. Have I told you about my hemorrhoids?

Lösung

	ENGLISCH		DEUTSCH
1	subtle	=	subtil, (feinfühlig, fein)
2	authentic	=	authentisch
3	banal	=	banal
4	card	≠	die (Speise-) Karte
5	controversial	=	kontrovers
	card	=	die Visitenkarte, Postkarte, der Karton
	the menu	=	**die (Speise-) Karte**

Richtig wäre:

Before my son's first visit to an expensive restaurant, I gave him a tip: if you can't think what to say, talk about something on the **menu**. Imagine his girlfriend's face when he said: "Did you see the dead fly on the Entrees page?"

50. Fashion news

1. Roberto Milano said his summer fashion collection was "a **synthesis** of 1930s chic and 1990s cool". In other words, it wasn't very original.

2. Long skirts might look like an **anachronism** but I wear them because fat legs have *never* been fashionable!

3. Josie Martin has been on the **periphery** of the fashion world for 10 years. But since Meg Ryan wore one of her hats, she's been this season's favorite designer.

4. The students at St Daniel's Art School have never been very **orthodox**. But this week, they all came to classes wearing dog coats and moccasins.

5. A leading UK fashion house has taken the unusual step of advertising for a new chief designer. It says it wants a young designer, probably aged 25 to 30, (**eventually** in their early 20s).The post became vacant when Zizzi le Troupe died after falling from her 27cm heels.

Lösung

	ENGLISCH		DEUTSCH
1	synthesis	=	die Synthese
2	anachronism	=	der Anachronismus
3	periphery	=	die Peripherie
4	orthodox	=	orthodox
5	eventually	≠	eventuell
	eventually	=	endlich, irgendwann einmal, letztendlich, schließlich
	possibly, maybe	=	**eventuell**

Richtig wäre:

A leading UK fashion house has taken the unusual step of advertising for a new chief designer. It says it wants a young designer, probably aged 25 to 30, (**possibly** in their early 20s). The post became vacant when Zizzi le Troupe died after falling from her 27cm heels.

The last think you would want to eat at a fine restaurant is the "menu" (= die Speisekarte). Better go for the "dish of the day", or the "chef's recommendation".

Some German speakers prefer an "s" sound to a "th" - "thick" becomes "sick", "thank" becomes "sank", and "thinking" becomes "sinking".

51. Strange behaviour

1. After my baby daughter was born, I became so **paranoid** about cleanliness that I even made the cat wash his face and paws before eating.

2. My mother is getting much more **extrovert** as she gets older. Yesterday, we went out to lunch and she started singing in the restaurant. Luckily, as I grow older, I'm getting more difficult to embarrass.

3. **My man** has been acting rather strange lately. Last night, he wore his gardening gloves with his best suit and put a slice of tomato in Hilda's gin and tonic.

4. One day, I got so angry with my manager that I threw a cream cake in his face. As a **consequence**, I lost my job but I soon got a new one … with the circus.

5. Mrs Craven has always been a bit **pedantic** but last week we actually saw her correcting the grammar in some graffiti on our office wall.

Lösung

	ENGLISCH		DEUTSCH
1	paranoid	=	paranoid
2	extrovert	=	extrovertiert
3	my man	≠	mein Mann
4	pedantic	=	pedantisch
5	consequence	=	die Konsequenz
	my man	=	mein Diener, Dienstbote
	my husband	=	**mein Mann**

Richtig wäre:

My husband has been acting rather strange lately. Last night, he wore his gardening gloves with his best suit and put a slice of tomato in Hilda's gin and tonic.

52. Wonders of the modern world

1. Today I saw a soft winter jacket made from old Coca-Cola bottles. I guess that's what you call 21st-century **alchemy!**

2. Like many **impotent** men, I'm really grateful for Viagra. Now I just wish the doctors could find something to cure my wife's headaches.

3. My American grandma telephoned to speak with Susan and I explained she'd gone shopping. "Why don't you call her **handy**," I suggested. Grandma, who's a little deaf, replied: "Why *should* I call her Andy?"

4. I was amazed by the revelation that **astronomers** had found ice on Mars. Some days, I have trouble finding it in my fridge.

5. You know you have 'computer **mania**' when you can remember more email addresses than phone numbers.

Lösung

	ENGLISCH		DEUTSCH
1	alchemy	=	die Alchemie
2	impotent	=	impotent
3	handy	≠	das Handy
4	astronomers	=	die Astronomen
5	mania	=	die Manie
	handy	=	praktisch, passend, griffig
	mobile (phone), cellular (phone)	=	**das Handy**

Richtig wäre:

My American grandma telephoned to speak with Susan and I explained she'd gone shopping. "Why don't you call her **mobile**," I suggested. Grandma, who's a little deaf, replied: "What did you say?"

53. Where do you spend the weekends?

1. We've had a caravan at Muckleton for 20 years. It's not meant to be a **static** one, but the wheels fell off in 1982 so we can't move it to a nicer place.

2. I always visit my cousin Peter at his restaurant on a Friday night. But my friendliness is just a **façade**, I really go to see him to get a free meal.

3. Valerie and I spend time helping foreigners at the **asylum** centre. We do it because these people need friends - and so do we.

4. I go to a Singles Club at Kleindorf. It's such good fun that I really don't want to meet a partner, because then I'd fail the only **criterion** for membership.

5. My wife hates it when I **stand up** early during the week, so at weekends we stay in bed until 11am - unless the grandkids are coming for lunch - then we stay in bed until they've gone!

Lösung

	ENGLISCH		DEUTSCH
1	static	=	statisch
2	façade	=	die Fassade
3	asylum	=	das Asyl
4	criterion	=	das Kriterium
5	stand up (early)	≠	(früh) aufstehen
	stand up early	=	in der Früh eine Erektion haben(!)
	get up early	=	**früh aufstehen**

Richtig wäre:

My wife hates it when I **get up** early during the week, so at weekends we stay in bed until 11am - unless the grandkids are coming for lunch - then we stay in bed until they've gone!

54. And the day had started so well ...

1. The telephone was quiet, my co-workers were away on business: in short, the office was as peaceful as a **cloister** – until the photocopier exploded.

2. I had arranged a **date** with my dentist this afternoon. When he handed me the bill, I was so shocked that my new teeth almost fell out.

3. I was so pleased that everyone at work had remembered my 50th birthday – until I found, among the cards on my desk, a note saying the firm was making all employees over 49 **redundant**.

4. At breakfast, my girlfriend told me she had never felt such **profound** love for someone. That night, she told me that the "someone" was someone else.

5. I finished translating the last sentence of the 600 page **manuscript** at 8am this morning. At 9am, I left it on the bus.

Lösung

	ENGLISCH		DEUTSCH
1	cloister	=	das Kloster
2	date	≠	das (Besprechungs-)Datum
3	redundant	=	redundant
4	profound	=	profund, (tief)
5	manuscript	=	das Manuskript
	date	=	Rendezvous, romantische Verabredung
	appointment, meeting	=	**das (Besprechungs-)Datum**

Richtig wäre:

I had arranged an **appointment** with my dentist this afternoon. When he handed me the bill, I was so shocked that my new teeth almost fell out.

55. "I can resist everything but temptation." (Oscar Wilde)

1. Jessica promised Jim that after they married she'd become a vegetarian like him. But when she saw what lovely **flesh** the butcher had last week she couldn't say "no" - so she got six kilos delivered to her office.

2. I was **resolute** about not having a relationship with anyone at work. But when you meet Justina, I think you'll agree that some rules are worth breaking.

3. Gavin says he can't **illustrate** my next cookery book. He's on a diet and says that drawing the pictures makes him hungry.

4. I was just about to leave the party when a **prominent** member of the Foreign Minister's team arrived. I had to stay and talk to her (about my company's plans to open a new factory in Malaysia). Well, it would have been rude not to, wouldn't it?

5. I'd like my **epitaph** to read: "She shopped until she dropped."

Lösung

	ENGLISCH		DEUTSCH
1	flesh	≠	das Fleisch (vom Tier)
2	resolute	=	resolut, (hier: entschlossen)
3	illustrate	=	illustrieren
4	prominent	=	prominent
5	epitaph	=	das Epitaph, (Grabinschrift)
	flesh	=	das menschliche Fleisch
	meat	=	**das Fleisch**

Richtig wäre:

Jessica promised Jim that after they married she'd become a vegetarian like him. But when she saw what lovely **meat** the butcher had last week she couldn't say "no" - so she got six kilos delivered to her office.

56. Some people are just difficult

1. Molly seemed **irritated** when I asked her if she had stolen the cakes. But as she stamped her foot, a strawberry éclair fell from her coat onto the floor.

2. Anthony can be so **irrational**. Last summer he wore his jumper to the beach every day. Now it's December and he's snowboarding in shorts.

3. Kate has been very **brusque** with me since I told her I couldn't come to her wedding. I think she is being very unfair because I did attend her previous three weddings.

4. Jake is a **undisciplined** child. The first words he said to me were: "I want to speak to your manager."

5. Nick's friends all think he's really **sympathetic** - but at home we see a different side. He uses bad language to his father and for Christmas he gave me a library book, due back on January 8.

Lösung

	ENGLISCH		DEUTSCH
1	irritated	=	irritiert
2	irrational	=	irrational
3	brusque	=	brüsk, schroff
4	undisciplined	=	undiszipliniert
5	sympathetic	≠	sympathisch
	sympathetic	=	mitfühlend, verständnisvoll
	nice, likeable, friendly	=	**sympathisch**

Richtig wäre:

Nick's friends all think he's really **nice** - but at home we see a different side. He uses bad language to his father and for Christmas he gave me a library book, due back on January 8.

57. Ours was a funny family

1. Dad said he wished that **bigamy** were legal in this country. With two wives, he thought he'd double his chance of remembering one wedding anniversary.

2. Auntie Edna was so keen to improve her cooking that whenever we visited her for lunch she asked us to complete a long **formula** about all aspects of the meal!

3. My family led a **nomadic** life; we were always moving house. That's why today I never go anywhere without my pyjamas.

4. Uncle Sam was totally **eccentric**. He used to wear a clean shirt and tie to bed every night. He said one never knew where one might go in a dream, and he wanted to be properly dressed if it was somewhere nice.

5. Mother always believed there was a **correlation** between eating a good breakfast and the ability to work well. I'm grateful that she cared for her children but I wish she wouldn't come to my office with bacon and eggs every morning.

Lösung

	ENGLISCH		DEUTSCH
1	bigamy	=	die Bigamie
2	formula	≠	das Formular
3	nomadic	=	nomadisch, (wie die Nomaden)
4	eccentric	=	exzentrisch
5	correlation	=	die Korrelation, (hier: Beziehung)
	formula	=	die Formel
	form, questionnaire	=	**das Formular**

Richtig wäre:

Auntie Edna was so keen to improve her cooking that whenever we visited her for lunch she asked us to complete a long **questionnaire** about all aspects of the meal!

In German your "Haus" can refer to your company or private location. Not so in English where "house" is always private. Talk about your "company", "firm", or "facility".

The English word "flesh" only refers to living human tissue. Only Hannibal Lector can say this convincingly! We recommend you say "I like to eat meat".

Pseudo-English

Es gibt „englische" Wörter, die zwar von Deutschsprechenden erfunden wurden, im Englischen in dieser Form aber gar nicht vorkommen. Diese nennt man anglisierende Bildungen bzw. Scheinentlehnungen. Manche dieser Wörter kommen zwar im englischen Sprachgebrauch vor - jedoch mit ganz anderer Bedeutung!

Behalten und vermeiden Sie die häufigsten 8 dieser Pseudo-Englisch Wörter:

1. **der Body** = bodysuit, body shirt, a tight-fitting one-piece garment for the torso (engl. body = der Körper)

2. **der Bodybag** = a bag that is carried on one strap across the body (engl. bodybag = der Leichensack)

3. **der Dress** = sport suit, special costume (engl. dress = Das Kleid)

4. **der Dressman** = male model (eng. dressman = ? ist unbekannt, auf engl. eventuell Transvestite)

5. **das Handy** = mobile phone, cell phone (engl. handy = praktisch, handlich)

6. **der Oldtimer** = vintage, veteran, classic car (engl. oldtimer = alter, erfahrener Mensch; Veteran)

7. **der Showmaster** = master of ceremonies, MC, show host (engl. showmaster = ?)

8. **der Smoking** = dinner jacket (UK), tuxedo, tux, black tie (US) (engl. smoking = rauchen)

Only German speakers call a "mobile phone" a "Handy" – thinking it's from the English. It's less traumatic to leave your "cellphone" or "mobile" at the reception!

Be very sure that you mean what you say - an "oldtimer" in English is an "old fellow" or an "old cowboy" - to describe cars choose the adjectives "classic", "vintage", or "veteran".

Sie denken *auf deutsch*	**Sie sagen** *auf englisch*	**Man versteht** *in UK und USA*	**Korrekt** *wäre*
Afrikaner	*African*	*ein Bure, ein Weißer*	Black African, African negro
Akkord	*accord*	*von selbst, von allein*	chord, piecework, agreement
akquirieren	*acquire*	*erwerben, bekommen*	look for, canvas for, get
Akquise, Akquisition	*acquisition*	*Erwerb, Erwerbung*	getting, securing
Aktion	*action*	*Tat, Handlung*	campaign, project programme
aktuell	*actual*	*tatsächlich, eigentlich, echt*	current, up to date, of interest today
Allee	*alley*	*Gäßchen, Gasse*	avenue
Ambulanz	*ambulance*	*Krankenwagen*	outpatients' department
Art	*art*	*Kunst*	way; manner, (personal) style
Auf die Damen!	*on the ladies!*	*An die Damen!*	To the ladies!
ausländisch	*outlandish*	*exotisch, fremdartig*	foreign
Baracke	*barracks*	*Kaserne*	(wooden) hut
bekommen	*become*	*werden*	get, receive
beraten	*berate*	*schelten, schimpfen*	advise, consult

Sie denken *auf deutsch*	**Sie sagen** *auf englisch*	**Man versteht** *in UK und USA*	**Korrekt** *wäre*
besiegen	*besiege*	*belagern*	defeat
Billion	*billion*	*Milliarde*	trillion
Biskuit	*biscuit*	*(GB) Keks; (US) kleines Brötchen*	sponge, sponge cake
sich blamieren	*blame*	*Schuld geben*	to make a fool of oneself
blutiges Steak	*bloody steak*	*verdammtes Steak*	rare steak
brav	*brave*	*tapfer*	good, well-behaved
Büro	*bureau*	*Sekretär (Möbel)*	office
Chef	*chef*	*Chefkoch*	boss
Chef	*chief*	*Häuptling*	boss
engagiert	*engaged*	*verlobt*	involved
eventuell	*eventually*	*schließlich, endlich*	perhaps
Fabrik	*fabric(s)*	*Stoff*	factory
Fahrt	*fart*	*furzen, Pups, Blähungen*	journey, trip
falsch	*false*	*unehrlich (false)*	wrong, incorrect

Sie denken *auf deutsch*	**Sie sagen** *auf englisch*	**Man versteht** *in UK und USA*	**Korrekt** *wäre*
familär	*familiar*	*bekannt*	personal
Fleisch	*flesh*	*menschliches Fleisch*	meat
Flur	*floor*	*Boden,*	hallway, entrance hall, corridor
Formular	*formula*	*Formel (chem., math.)*	questionnaire, form
freuen	*afraid*	*Angst haben*	to be happy, enjoy
(früh) aufstehen	*stand up (early)*	*sex. Erregung (männlich!)*	get up (early)
Gewinn	*win*	*gewinnen*	profit
Gift	*gift*	*Geschenk*	poison
glücklich	*lucky*	*Glück haben*	happy, cheerful
Gratifikation	*gratification*	*Befriedigung (sexuell)*	bonus
groß	*great*	*großartig, bedeutend*	big, large
gültig	*guilty*	*schuldig*	valid
Guten Appetit!	*good appetite*	*Essen Sie viel?*	bon appetit, (oder nichts sagen)
Haare	*hairs*	*Schamhaare*	hair

Sie denken *auf deutsch*	**Sie sagen** *auf englisch*	**Man versteht** *in UK und USA*	**Korrekt** *wäre*
Handy	*handy*	*praktisch, griffig*	*mobile, cellular phone*
Haus (Firma)	*house*	*Privat-Haus*	company, office
Justiz	*justice*	*Recht*	law
(Land-) Karte	*card*	*Visitenkarte*	map
Karte (Restaurant)	*card*	*Visitenkarte*	menu
Kaution	*caution*	*Vorsicht*	deposit
konsequent	*consequent*	*folgend*	consistent
Konstruktion (Fabrik)	*construction*	*Aufbau*	assembly
kontrollieren	*control*	*steuern, lenken*	check, test, examine
krank	*crank*	*Kurbel; alter Spinner*	sick, ill, unwell
Kritik	*critic*	*Kritiker*	criticism
Landschaft	*landscape*	*Gemälde-landschaft*	countryside, scenery
Lust	*lust*	*Begierde (sexuell)*	longing, liking for
Mappe	*map*	*Landkarte*	folder

Sie denken *auf deutsch*	Sie sagen *auf englisch*	Man versteht *in UK und USA*	Korrekt *wäre*
Marmelade	*marmalade*	*Orangen-marmelade*	jam
Mein Mann	*my man*	*mein Butler, Diener (Slang)*	my husband
Meine Frau	*my woman*	*Frau/Freundin (Slang)*	my wife
Meinung	*mean*	*Bedeutung*	opinion
Menü	*menu*	*Speisekarte*	fixed dishes selection
Mist	*mist*	*Nebel, Dunst*	dung, fertilizer, manure
muß nicht	*must not*	*darf nicht*	needn't don't have to
Mutterfirma	*mother company*	*?*	head office, HQ parent company,
Note (Schule)	*note*	*Notiz; Musiknote*	mark, grade
Oldtimer	*oldtimer*	*alter Mann*	classic car, veteran car, vintage car
ordinär	*ordinary*	*normal, nichts besonderes,*	vulgar, rude
Personal	*personal*	*persönlich*	personnel, staff, employees
Phantasie	*fantasy*	*Phantasie (sexuell)*	imagination
Präservativ	*preservative*	*Konservierungs-stoff*	condom

Sie denken *auf deutsch*	**Sie sagen** *auf englisch*	**Man versteht** *in UK und USA*	**Korrekt** *wäre*
Probe	*probe*	*Sonde*	test, trial, sample
Privater Teil (Haus)	*private part(s)*	*Geschlechts-organe*	living quarters
Prokurist, Prokura	*procurer*	*Zuhälter*	Manager with power of attorney
Prospekte	*prospects*	*Aussichten*	brochures
Provisionen	*provisions*	*Lebensmittel*	Commission
Prozess (jur.)	*process*	*Verfahren, Vorgang*	case, action, trial
prüfen	*prove*	*beweisen*	check
Raten (Geld)	*rates*	*Grundsteuer, Sätze*	instalments
rentabel	*rentable*	*zu vermieten*	lucrative, profitable
Rente	*rent*	*Miete*	pension
Ressort	*resort*	*Urlaubsort*	department
Rezept (med.)	*recipe*	*Kochrezept*	prescription
(Koch-) Rezept	*receipt*	*Quittung*	recipe
Rückseite	*backside*	*Hintern, Hinterteil, Po*	back, other side, reverse side

Sie denken *auf deutsch*	**Sie sagen** *auf englisch*	**Man versteht** *in UK und USA*	**Korrekt** *wäre*
sensibel	*sensible*	*vernünftig*	sensitive
seriös	*serious*	*ernst*	trustworthy
sinnvoll	*sinful*	*sündhaft*	meaningful
Smoking	*smoking*	*rauchen*	black tie, tuxedo (US)
sparen	*spare*	*Ersatz*	save
spendieren	*spend*	*ausgeben, verbringen*	donate, give
sympathisch	*sympathetic*	*mitfühlend*	nice, likeable
Technik	*technique*	*Methode*	technology
Termin	*date*	*Verabredung*	appointment, meeting
Unternehmer	*undertaker*	*Leichenbestatter*	entrepreneur
Warenhaus	*warehouse*	*Lagerhaus*	department store
wenn (falls)	*when*	*wenn, sobald (100% sicher)*	if
wollen	*will*	*werden*	want

As German speakers sometimes shock the British, so do the British the Americans. A "Radiergummi" = "rubber" in the UK; but in the US "rubber" = "condom"! In America, it's better to ask for an "eraser".

The British will "knock you up" (jmd aufwecken) whenever you like. This is not appreciated in the States where "knock-up" means "jdm schwängern".

Instant English

Ein Trick zur schnellen Erweiterung anspruchsvollen Englischvokabulars ist der Gebrauch identischer Wörter!
Da Sie jetzt mit den kritischsten Übersetzungsfehlern vertraut sind, stehen Ihnen tausende von identischen und ähnlichen, deutschen Wörter auch im Englischen zur freien Verfügung.
Die folgende Liste enthält typische „Instant"-Wörter, mit denen Sie sofort Ihren Wortschatz aufpeppen können.
Beachten Sie dabei, dass im amerikanischen und britischen Sprachgebrauch mitunter auch deutsche Wörter vorkommen.

absolute
abseil
abstract
accent
accept
acquisition
acute
adapt
aesthetic
alchemy
alibi
allegory
amateur
amnesty
amortization
anachronism
analysis
anarchy
angst
anecdote
anonymous
anthology
apathy
archives
arguments
aristocratic
arrogant
assimilate
astronomer
asylum
atheist
authentic
autobahn
autocratic
autonomous
aversion

Instant English

balance
banal
bastion
Bauhaus
bigamy
blitzkrieg
bonus
bourgeois
bratwurst
burg
bravado
brusque
Bundesbank
bureaucracy
cabal
capitalism
caricature
catastrophe
categorical
channel
charisma
charlatan
chronic
chronological
classic
cliché
climate
cloister
coffee-klatsch
coalition
comment
communicate
compatible
compensate
compromise
concept
conflict
consequence
consolidate
consonant
consterned
contraband
controversial
conundrum
conventional
correlation
corrupt
cosmopolitan
crisis
criterion
criticism
dachshund
debacle
debate
decadent
defensive
definitive
degenerate
degrade
demarcation
demographic
despot
diagnose
didactic
dilemma
dilettante
direct
disaster
discipline
discrepancy
discriminate
dissident
doberman
dogmatic
doppelganger

Instant English

doppler effect
dubious
dummkopf
eccentric
echo
ecological
efficient
egocentric
elegant
elite
eloquent
emancipation
embargo
energy
epitaph
equivalent
ersatz
esoteric
ethical
euphemism
euphoria
eventually
exclusive
experimental
explicit
exquisite
extrovert
façade
fatal
fiasco
flagrant
fragment
freudian
frugal
Geiger counter
generate
genre
gemütlich (US)
gestalt
gesticulate
gesundheit! (US)
glockenspiel
hamster
harmony
hedonism
heresy
heterogeneous
hierarchy
horizon
horizontal
humbug
hypothesis
ideology
idiomatic
idiosyncrasy
idiosyncratic
idyllic
ignore
illusion
illustrate
immigration
impotent
improvise
incognito
indifferent
infobahn
infrastructure
innovation
inquisition
insolent
insolvency
inspection
intimate
introvert
ironic

Instant English

irritated
jargon
Junta
Kapellmeister
kaputt
kindergarten
labyrinth
laconic
lager beer
lament
latent
Lebensraum
lederhosen
leitmotiv
litany
lobby
mania
manuscript
masochist
materialistic
maxim
medium
mentor
metamorphosis
miniature
mobilise
monotonous
morally
motif
muesli
neanderthal
nepotism
neutral
nomadic
nominal
nonchalant
nostalgia
oasis
objective
offensive
ominous
optimistic
opulent
orthodox
pacifists
panorama
paradox
parallel
paranoid
parasites
pedantic
periphery
perverse
pessimistic
philanthropy
phlegmatic
pils, pilsner
platonic
plausible
plunder
pluralism
polemic
poltergeist
pretzel
precise
profound
prognosis
prominent
protégé
prudent
qualify
rational
reaction
redundant
regime

Instant English

reincarnation
religious
renovate
reserved
reserves
resolute
rigorous
risk
robust
romantic
rottweiler
rucksack
rustic
scandal
sauerkraut
schadenfreude
schnapps
schnitzel
sect
sensation
situation
skeptical
solidarity
special
spectrum
sporadic
spritzer
static
sterile
strike
strudel
subjective
subtle
superlative
symmetry
synchronize
synonym
synthesis
tactical
tirade
tragic
transfer
transient
trauma
travesty
undisciplined
verboten
virtuous
waltz
wanderlust
wunderkind
yodel
zeitgeist

In the UK "Hosen" = trousers, in the US "Hosen" = pants. In the UK "pants" = "Unterhosen"! No wonder that the British sometimes worry if their American cousins will arrive properly dressed.

"Prokurist" does not translate easily into English. Don't even think about saying "I'm a procurer" – unless you're responsible for the girls. Procurer = Zuhälter.

English Good Times & Bad Times

„My problem with English …“ lamentieren viele Deutsche, „… is with the times.“ „That's quite understandable …,“ antworten wir, „… The Times can be a difficult newspaper to understand, even for many non-Native speakers.“

Britische Zeitungen sind aber nicht gemeint. Die Anwendung englischer Zeitformen ist es, was vielen Deutschen Kopfzerbrechen bereitet.

Glücklicherweise gibt es ein einfaches System, das man bei ca. 80% der englischen Sätze anwenden kann. Sobald Sie dieses Konzept verstehen, können Sie sicher sein, dass Ihre Sprachkenntnisse eine solide Basis haben.

Wenn Sie die nächsten Seiten lesen, werden Sie die häufigsten, typischen Übersetzungsfehler der Zeitformen verstehen - Ihre Kenntnis der englischen Grammatik wird gefestigter sein als die vieler Ihrer Kollegen.

Bitte nehmen Sie sich ein oder zwei Minuten Zeit für den folgenden Test, bevor Sie weiterlesen.

Fügen Sie die korrekte englische Verbform in die Lücken der unten stehenden Sätze ein.

1. Peter (*hat studiert*) ______________ in Oxford.

2. They (*arbeiten*) ______________ in sales at our Frankfurt office.

3. Just a moment, he (*spricht*) ______________ on the other line.

4. That's Mr Meyer, he (*arbeitete*) ______________ for the company for over 20 years.

5. Claudia (*hat besucht*) ______________ Tokyo last year.

6. Hans (*wohnt*) ______________ in a village south of Munich.

7. At the moment our main competitor (*verkauft*) ____________ 20% more than us.

8. I love golf. I (*spiele*) ______________ since the early 1980's.

9. I (*habe gesehen*) ______________ the general manager yesterday.

10. We (*produzieren*) ______________ chemicals for the plastics' industry.

11. Take care, that machine (*läuft*) ______________ too fast!

12. For many years now we (*einkaufen*) ______________ components from China.

Bevor Sie Ihre Antworten überprüfen, vergleichen wir kurz die englischen Zeitformen mit den deutschen.

Das Englische kennt sehr viele verschiedene Zeitformen (allein schon neun Varianten im Futur!) - aber keine Angst, Sie brauchen längst nicht alle zu beherrschen.

Bei der Analyse britischer oder amerikanischer Zeitungen, Radio- oder Fernsehsendungen werden Sie feststellen, dass ca. 80% des geschriebenen und gesprochenen Englisch aus nur vier verschiedenen Zeiten besteht.

Interessanterweise sind es genau diese vier Zeitformen, die den meisten Deutschsprachigen Schwierigkeiten bereiten, wenn sie englisch sprechen oder schreiben.

Die Konsequenzen können gravierend sein. So könnte z.B. Ihr Geschäftspartner davon ausgehen, dass Sie eigentlich die Gegenwart meinen, während Sie glauben sich in der Vergangenheit auszudrücken.

Unser dringender Rat: Eignen Sie sich die 80% der häufigsten Zeitformen sicher an - über die restlichen 20% können Sie sich später Gedanken machen.

Wir haben vier der wichtigsten Zeiten für Sie visulaisiert dargestellt, damit Sie sich diese leichter einprägen und im Gedächtnis behalten können:

1. The Dinosaur
(oder „The Simple Past"/ einfache Vergangenheit)

- I saw him last night.
- He was born in London in 1950.
- The plane landed 10 minutes ago.

Für die einfache Vergangenheit (Simple Past) visualisieren Sie einfach einen „**Dinosaur**". Dinosaurier existieren nicht mehr, sie sind tot, sie sind ausgestorben. Denken Sie an irgendeinen Satz, der sich auf ein *abgeschlossenes Ereignis in der Vergangenheit* bezieht. Auf Deutsch benutzen wir meist „haben" und „sein" , wenn wir uns auf den **Dinosaur** beziehen:

- Ich *habe* ihn gestern abend gesehen.
- Er *ist* in London in 1950 geboren.
- Die *Maschine* ist vor 10 Minuten gelandet.

Bitte prägen Sie sich ein, dass im Englischen NICHT „sein" und „haben" genommen wird, um auf eine abgeschlossene Situation hinzuweisen – das wäre ein typisch deutscher Übersetzungsfehler.

Überprüfen Sie jetzt Ihre Verbform-Antworten der Sätze 1., 5., und 9.

1. They *lived* (nicht "have lived") in London in 1985.
5. Claudia *visited* (nicht "has visited") Tokyo last year.
9. I *saw* (nicht "have seen") the general manager yesterday.

Sie können die **Dinosaur**-Sätze leicht im Englischen erkennen an der Verwendung von

a. „haben" und „sein" im Deutschen, und
b. auf die Vergangenheit verweisender Indikatoren wie :"yesterday"; "last" night/week/month ...; 5 minutes, 10 days, 20 years "ago"; und abgeschlossenen Zeiträumen wie: 1978, 16th century, 250 A.D.

2. The Heart
(oder Simple Present/ einfache Gegenwart)

- I love Mozart
- He runs the personnel department
- They all live within 50 miles of central London

Für die einfache Gegenwart (Simple Present) stellen Sie sich einfach ein **„Heart“** vor. Das Herz erinnert uns an Liebe, und Liebe ist für immer. **Heart**-Sätze stehen für einen konstanten, stetigen Status.

Wenn wir uns über uns, unseren Beruf, unsere Firma, unsere Meinung oder die allgemeine Lage äußern, müssen wir die **Heart**-Form nehmen.

An etwas unter der Voraussetzung „wie oft“ zu denken ist ein guter Weg die **Heart**-Form zu verstehen. Wenn Wörte wie “always, never, sometimes, usually, seldom, often, ...” in Ihren Sätzen vorkommen – benutzen Sie die **Heart**-Form.

Der typische Fehler bei dieser Grammatikform ist die Benutzung der “Verlaufsform”. Bitte nicht “ING” an Ihr Verb “hängen”, wenn es sich um irgendeinen andauernden Zustand handelt.

Überprüfen Sie jetzt Ihre Verbform-Antworten der Sätze 2., 6. und 10.

2. Peter *works* (nicht ‘is working’) for us at our Frankfurt office.
6. Hans *lives* (nicht ‘is living’) in a village south of Munich.
10. We *produce* (nicht ‘are producing’) chemicals for the plastics’ industry.

3. The Cloud

(oder „Present Continuous"/ Verlaufsform)

- It's raining in London
- We are staying in the Hilton Hotel
- This project is running for the next 3 months

Für die Verlaufsformen (present continuous) stellen Sie sich eine Wolke vor. Diese symbolisiert das Wetter, das sich immer ändert und ständig in Bewegung ist.

Wenn ein Ereignis oder eine Handlung befristet oder absehbar vorübergehend ist, wird im Englischen die Verlaufsform (... ing) eingesetzt. Dabei kann es sich um einen sehr kurzen Zeitabschnitt handeln (ein paar Sekunden) oder einen längeren Zeitraum (einige Monate). Das Wesentliche bei der **Cloud**-Form ist, dass Sie das Ende einer Situation absehen können. Typische Indikatoren für das **Cloud**-System sind Wörter wie: "now; at the moment; currently; today; at present" und der Einsatz von "this" in Verbindung mit "week, month, year ...".

Überprüfen Sie jetzt Ihre Verbform-Antworten der Sätze 3., 7. und 11.

3. Just a moment, he *is speaking* (nicht 'speaks') on the other line.
7. At the moment our main competitor *is selling* (nicht 'sells') 20% more than we are.
11. Take care, that machine *is running* (nicht 'runs') too fast!

4. The Bridge
(oder „Present Perfect")

- I have known Jim for many years.
- We have owned this car since 1992.
- The company has been producing these units for over 10 years.

Das Present Perfect ist eine besonders interessante Variante, da es im Deutschen für diese Form kein direktes Äquivalent gibt. Die **Bridge**-Form (mit "have" oder "has" + Past Participle des Verbs) verbindet die Vergangenheit mit der Gegenwart und drückt „wie lange schon" aus oder „seit wann", also wann etwas seinen Anfang genommen hat und (seitdem) immer noch aktuell ist.

Wenn ein Ereignis, eine Handlung oder Situation in der Vergangenheit angefangen hat und noch andauert – „is still going" oder es ist gerade beendet und man spürt noch die Nachwirkungen, dann ist die **Bridge** die korrekte Zeitform. Aber viele Deutschsprachige wissen das nicht – sie benutzen irrtümlicherweise die continuous form (**Cloud**) statt der **Bridge**.

Überprüfen Sie jetzt Ihre Verbform-Antworten der Sätze 4., 8. und 12. mit dem Present Continous zuvor – Sie haben doch nicht etwa **Cloud** eingesetzt?

4. That's Mr Meyer, he *has worked* (nicht 'is working') for the company for over 20 years.
8. I love golf. I *have played* (nicht 'am playing') since the early1980's.
12. For many years now *we have bought* (nicht 'are buying') components from China.

Typische Indikatoren für die **Bridge**-Form sind die Präpositionen „since“ und „for“. Korrekterweise benutzt man „since“ mit festen Zeitangaben und „for“ für Zeitspannen:

- We have known them *since* 1980.
- He has been here *since* nine o'clock.
- We have known them *for* over 20 years.
- He has been here *for* 2 hours.

Ihr Lösungsprofil:

Mit welchen englischen Verb-Formen haben Sie typisch deutsche Fehler gemacht? Machen Sie einen Kreis um diese Fehler, um zu sehen auf welche Grammatikform Sie besonders achten sollten.

Simple Past	Simple Present	Present Continuous	Present Perfect

1	**2**	**3**	**4**
5	**6**	**7**	**8**
9	**10**	**11**	**12**

Fehler-Auswertung:

8 – 12 Fehler = Durchschnittliches Ergebnis. Sie befinden sich in guter Gesellschaft - ca. 50% der Deutschsprachigen, die diesen Test machen, befinden sich in dieser Kategorie.

5 – 7 Fehler = Überdurchschnittlich. Die Wahl Ihrer englischen Zeitformen ist gut, aber Sie denken noch „auf Deutsch".

0 – 4 Fehler = Exzellentes Ergebnis. Auf diesem Niveau verstehen Sie auch die Zeitformfehler, die Ihre deutschsprachigen Kollegen und ausländischen Geschäftspartner machen.

Was nun?

Wie war das Testergebnis? Falls es nicht so gut ausfiel, machen Sie sich keine Sorgen. Sie sind in guter Gesellschaft - viele, die wir testen, irren sich bei mehr als 50% dieser Verb-Formen.

Die zwei häufigsten Fehler, auf die man achten sollte, sind:

1. Das deutsche "haben/sein" direkt ins Englische zu übersetzen und die **Bridge**-Zeitform einzusetzen.

Wenn Sie ausdrücken möchten, dass ein Event vorbei ist - richtig wäre der "**Dinosaur**" - wählen Sie oft (falsch!) die **Bridge**, und infolgedessen verstehen Englischsprachige "immer noch". Ein einfacher und logischer Fehler, der leicht zu korrigieren ist, wenn man ihn einmal verstanden hat.

2. Die ing-Form (**Cloud**) zu bevorzugen, wenn man in der Gegenwart spricht.

Das Present Continuous ist die beliebteste der Zeiten, die man in vielen englischen Unterrichtsstunden zuerst lernt. Die **Cloud** hat Vorteile - sie ist leicht zu unterrichten und zu lernen, und sie wirkt anspruchsvoll und kultiviert:

- Michael is working for Siemens.
- Michael isn't working for Siemens
- Is Michael working for Siemens?
- Isn't Michael working for Siemens?

Das Ergebnis dieses **Cloud**-Unterrichts ist, dass viele sehr darauf fixiert sind und diese Zeitform bei (fast) jeder Gelegenheit benutzen. Was viele aber nicht berücksichtigen ist, dass sich dann die Bedeutung ändert:

a Michael arbeitet (works) bei Siemens (festes Arbeitsverhältnis) im Unterschied zu
b Michael arbeitet (is working) bei Siemens (absehbarer Zeitraum, z.B. er hat bereits gekündigt)

Analysieren Sie eine britische oder amerikanische Zeitung oder Magazin oder hören Sie "Native Speakers" zu – Sie werden feststellen, dass **Cloud** in der Gegenwartsform ziemlich selten vorkommt – in etwa 90% der Gegenwartsform wird **Heart** genommen!

Wenn man über die Vergangenheit spricht, sind die meisten englischen Sätze einfache **Dinosaurs**, während Deutschsprachige aus den erwähnten Gründen **Clouds** und **Bridges** wählen.

Die Statistik

Einsatz der Zeitformen in der allgemeinen Konversation (in Prozent):

Bridge "I *have done* my best" – **ca. 5%**

Cloud "I *am doing* my best" – **ca. 10%**

Dinosaur "I *did* my best" – **ca. 20%**

Heart "I *do* my best" – **ca. 45%**

ALL THE REST – ca. 20%
z.B. "If I had known then what I know now, I wouldn't have spent so much time on English grammar."

Der wichtigste Tipp:

Das Entscheidende für jeden, der interessiert ist an einer pragmatischen Lehrmethode der englischen Grammatik, ist Folgendes:
Benutzen Sie **Dinosaur** und **Heart** wann immer möglich - Ihre Grammatik wird in den meisten Fällen richtig sein!

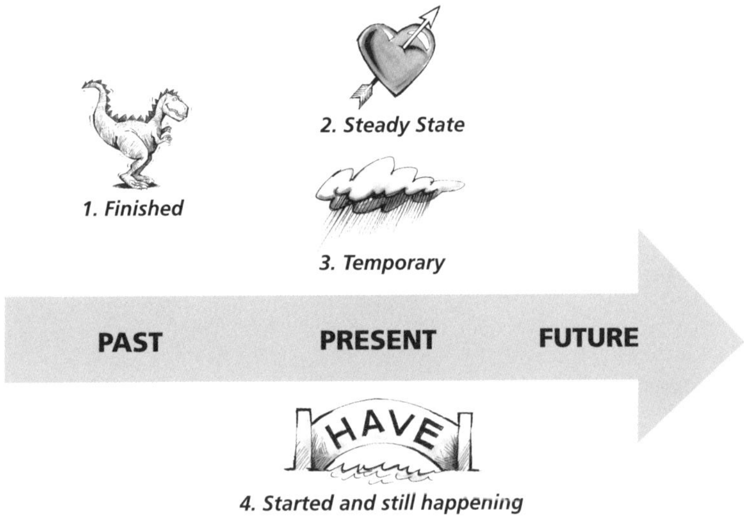

Die restlichen 20%

Was ist aber mit den restlichen 20% der englischen Grammatik? Dem Futur? Den Conditionals? Dem Past Perfect? Dies sind alles wichtige Zeitformen, kein Zweifel. Andererseits, sollten Sie die vielfältigen Futurformen verwechseln oder ein falsches Conditional benutzen, ist das Potenzial für *gravierende* Missverständnisse immer noch minimal.

Falls Sie aber dennoch Zeit und Interesse haben sollten, Ihre Grammatik perfektionieren zu wollen, empfehlen wir Ihnen das Nachschlagewerk der Englischlehrer: "Practical English Usage" (s. Referenzteil).

Referenzen

Es gibt ca. 500 knifflige Wörter (false-friends), die Ihre deutsch-englische Kommunikation stören könnten - wir haben die wichtigsten davon abgedeckt. Wenn Sie sich mit diesem Thema intensiver beschäftigen möchten, insbesondere wenn Sie Englisch oder Deutsch unterrichten, empfehlen wir Ihnen folgendes:

1. Sprachfallen Englisch - Graham Pascoe, Henriette Pascoe (Hueber)
2. Can I become a beefsteak? - Margaret Helliwell (Cornelsen & OUP)
3. Practical English Usage - Michael Swan (OUP)

PSA-Service:
Das kostenlose „One-Word-A-Day" und Checklisten, z.B. deutsche Wörter, die man auch im Englischen benutzt, finden Sie bei: www.owad.de

Danke!

Ein ganz großes Dankeschön an Lis Ribbans, deren journalistische Fähigkeiten und Sinn für Humor Sie in den Beispielsätzen des Quiz finden.

Vera F. Birkenbihl, einer lieben Freundin und Kollegin, deren Kreativität und Humor immer eine große Inspiration sind, ein herzliches „Danke für alles, Vera!".

Und natürlich ein ganz besonderes Dankeschön an unsere internationalen-Freunde, Kollegen und Geschäftspartner die - meist unfreiwillig - dazu beigetragen haben, diese "Fehler"-Sammlung überhaupt zu ermöglichen …
… während die Autoren selbst jede Anstrengung auf sich genommen haben, Fehler zu vermeiden, but … nobody's perfect …

Helga & Paul Smith, Bernhard Förth

Autoren

Helga & Paul Smith

Helga und Paul Smith leiten PSA International - a creative consulting firm supporting top companies worldwide with innovative corporate events and management development programmes.

The authors' observations at numerous international conferences, seminars and workshops have provided much of the raw material for this book.

More about Helga, Paul & PSA under: *www.psa-international.com*

Bernhard Förth

Typograph und Graphik-Designer
Seit 1983 freier Illustrator

Tätig in den Bereichen Jugendbuch, Karikatur, Cartoon in vielseitigen Techniken. Auftraggeber sind Buchverlage, Zeitschriftenverlage, Industrie sowie Privatkunden. Bernhard Förth arbeitet auch privat im künstlerischen Bereich und konnte seine Werke innerhalb einiger Sammel- wie auch Einzelausstellungen zeigen.